THE LIFE AND TIMES

OF

MAX PINE

A History of the Jewish Labor Movement in the U.S.A. during the last part of the 19th Century and the first part of the 20th Century

By

HYMAN J. FLIEGEL

Counsel to Bnai Zion
The American Fraternal Zionist Organization

Published by HYMAN J. FLIEGEL
285 Madison Avenue, New York City

i

Dedicated to my dear wife, Mollie,
and my dear daughter, Sylvia Nachtigall

FOREWORD

LETTER OF YITZHAK BEN ZVI, PRESIDENT
OF THE STATE OF ISRAEL, TO THE AUTHOR

STATE OF ISRAEL
Le President De L'etat D'Israel

Jerusalem, 10, Menachim Av, 5678
July 27, 1958

Mr. Hyman J. Fliegel
New York

Dear Mr. Fliegel:

I was happy to receive your letter of July 3, 1958, together with the proofs of your book dedicated to the distinguished leader of Jewish labor in the United States, Max Pine.

I had the honor and pleasure of associating with Pine and was his beneficiary during my mission in America at the beginning of 1926, on behalf of the Histadruth campaign, of which I was one of the organizers. I was always deeply impressed by the devotion and the extraordinary zeal of Max Pine. I admired the youthful energy displayed by this grey-headed man. He was able to penetrate our spirit and wisely understood our soul. He was whole-heartedly identified with the proletariat of Eretz Yisroel.

The personality of Pine served as a shining example to many. He was of the select few who knew how to bridge the gulf that separated the Jewish laborer in America from the working masses that dwelled in Zion.

The men of the Histadruth and all the people that dwell in Israel knew how to cherish Pine's devoted service. They manifested their admiration for him by naming a group of vocational schools in Eretz Yisroel after him so that his name is now mentioned with gratitude by tens of thousands of the House of Israel.

I congratulate your initiative in writing this book. I felicitate the Chavarim who are helping to publish and spread this book among our brothers and friends.

With great esteem,

/s/ Y. Ben Zvi

YITZHAK BEN ZVI

Letter translated from Hebrew to English by Dr Joseph Miller, Rabbi of Congregation Shaare Torah of Flatbush and former President of the New York Board of Rabbis.

v

TABLE OF CONTENTS

THE LIFE AND TIMES OF MAX PINE

———◆———

Chapter 1

PERSONALITY

The news of Pine's death stirred the New York worker as though each had suffered the loss of his own brother. Funeral services were held at the Forward Hall on March 4, 1928. Between March 2, when he died, and the services, he lay in state and thousands passed his bier to honor him. Rutgers Square, on which the Forward Building fronted, was filled with people. In the Hall itself were representatives of national labor unions and Jewish institutions. Abraham Cahan, editor of the Forward; M. Tygel, chairman of the United Hebrew Trades; B. Vladek, manager of the Forward; B. Zuckerman, on behalf of the Geverkshaften Campaign; Judge Jacob Panken; David Hoze, labor leader of Palestine, representing the Histradut; Morris Sigman, president of the International Ladies' Garment Workers' Union; Joseph Schlossberg, Secretary of the Amalgamated Clothing Workers' Union; H. Weinberg, President of the Workman's Circle; Rubin Guskin, Manager of the Jewish Theatrical Union; I. Roberts, Secretary of the International Capmakers' Union, etc.; Herbert H. Lehman and Felix Warburg were amongst a group of notables in the audience.

The eulogies covered the many-sided facets of Pine's career in the creation and development of the trade-union movement in America, about the idealism and self-sacrifice he showed in all his activities; about his devotion to the relief activity; and lastly, about the courage he showed in creating the Geverkshaften Campaign.

Abraham Cahan, in speaking about him with pathos, proclaimed:

"Comrades, here lies a man who five years ago pioneered the movement to assist Jewish Labor in Palestine; he created it with great courage, enthusiasm and devotion. Many of us opposed him, but he finally succeeded and the work which he started is a great success. That same spirit and courage he exhibited in every one of his varied activities during the 40 years of his highly useful life.

"Comrades, here lies the person who abolished the sweat shops."

Vladek, in his eulogy, said:

"Comrade Pine was during his entire life like a beautiful flower surrounded with prickly thorns, and now, when his body is dead, like a burned bush, he is surrounded with sweet smelling flowers.

"Max Pine didn't have a single happy day. I don't believe he had even one week's vacation in his entire life. He ceaselessly worked for the labor movement.

"Between these narrow black-draped walls of the coffin lies forty years of Jewish Labor Movement in America, not a labor movement of drama and coffee salons, but one saturated with sweat, blood, daily cares and struggles.

"No person is a greater, more impressive symbol of the Jewish Labor struggle than is Max Pine.

"He fought for the workers and with the workers even way back when they carried their machines on their shoulders and ate their lunch

hanging from strings over their machines * * *
Max Pine led them to a better more healthy life.

"He led the Jewish laborer from the sweatshop to the unions that became an example for the
labor movement in all America."

After the eulogies, the coffin was carried out on the
shoulders of the officers of the United Hebrew Trades and
of the Geverkshaften Campaign. Following the funeral
car were thousands of mourners. The Forward set the
number at 10,000 and the New York Times at 4,000. The
procession led from the Forward Building through the
streets of the East Side and up Second Avenue. At Fourth
Street, the procession halted and a number of musicians
representing the Jewish Theatrical Union played taps.

At Mt. Carmel Cemetery where the interment took place,
additional eulogies were delivered by Isaac Hamlin on
behalf of the Paole Zion, Abraham Miller on behalf of the
Amalgamated Clothing Workers, and Alexander Rose on
behalf of the International Millinery Union.

The New York Times of March 5th, 1928, gave a full
account of the funeral services and the procession. The
report contained the following:

"Abraham Cahan extolled the fight Mr. Pine
carried on for more than forty years to improve
the conditions of the workers of the lower East
Side. *He gave Mr. Pine credit* for abolishing the
East Side sweatshops."

The first page of the New York Daily News carried a
large picture of the Pine funeral procession under the
heading: "East Side Honors Labor Leader".

* * *

Max Pine was born in 1866 in Liubavitch, a small town in the State of Mohlive, Russia. His father soon died and Max was sent by his mother to his aunt in Wielitch, State of Vitebsk, Russia, at the age of three. There he was raised and learned to be a typesetter. He had an uneventful childhood. He worked at his trade, married and was a very happy man when his son Harry was born.

Seeing no future in Czarist Russia, like many others of his generation, Pine set out for the "Golden Land"— America. He arrived here in 1890. At first he worked as a carrier of coal, walking to the fifth floor with a pail of coal on his shoulders. Then he became a knee-pants' operator. Soon he saved enough money with which to send for his wife and child, who arrived here on July 4, 1891. While he was working in a shop on the fourth floor of a Hester Street building, he used to bring his son Harry to the shop. Harry used to play in a large box which contained remnants, cloth, buttons, etc.

Work was generally seasonal. Some days there was work the first hour in the morning and then again for an hour in the afternoon. While waiting for work to resume, the workers amused themselves by playing card games known as "21", Casino and "Ocke". They also spent time in discussions. Pine had time to reflect and determined to improve the conditions of the workers. As he looked at the machine and the needle, he looked beyond them to better days for the persons at the machine.

He soon became the leader of the Knee-Pants Makers' Union. When he spoke to his union men or workers generally, he did not speak down to them but as one of them. He spoke from his heart and thus became beloved by all the workers. He worked with that union until the Forward was founded in 1897. He was then engaged by the Forward at $14.00 per week. He wrote for the paper and generally assisted in its preparation. He brought the type to the printer who was then on Duane Street, brought back the printed papers to Rutgers Square, and helped distribute them to the dealers.

In 1901 Pine went into the printing business on Allen Street. In 1903 he became a partner of one Schreiber and moved his business to Broome Street. In 1904 the partnership was dissolved and with his son, Harry, who was then 15, he opened a print shop in the cellar at 417 Grand Street.

During all of this time Pine delivered many addresses, speaking practically every evening and many times during the day. He helped organize new union shops and also spoke at Socialist Party meetings.

In 1903 Pine was Socialist Party candidate for the New York State Assembly for the 4th Assembly District—John Hunter was the candidate in the 6th, and Phelps Stokes in the 8th, all on the East Side. The campaign was bitter but unsuccessful in each instance.

In 1905 the print shop was moved to the stoop store at 12 Jefferson Street, which was an interesting building, for on the third floor there lived the great Nazimova and Olenoff and their theatrical troupe which made appearances at the Little Theatre on 3rd Street, just East of the Bowery. Pine helped the troupe greatly.

He gave up business in 1906 to become the Secretary and Executive Director of the United Hebrew Trades. As Secretary he received a salary of $40.00 per week. When he concluded the successful bakers' strike of 1909, the largest and most important strike till then, he resigned as Secretary and again with his son, went into the printing business. In the meantime he helped in the strikes of the waistmakers, furriers, ladies' garment workers, and others.

Soon it became necessary to organize the men's clothing industry, and the men's clothing workers—the tailors. Pine was chosen to organize them. He was told that the tailors could never be organized, could never get together and would never agree to strike because "Zai zainen nit kaiu mentchen.'' Once at Stuyvesant Casino on Second Avenue and St. Marks Place, Pine addressed a meeting of pressers, most of whom had gray beards. His son Harry described how his father took these pressers by storm. He told them what he was told about them. He then declared over and over again, ''I want to tell the whole world that tailors are people'' (schnaider zainen mentchen). The response was most enthusiastic, and on December 30, 1912, the ''Strike Hagodol''—the great tailor strike—was called by Pine. The impossible had been accomplished. The rest is history.

At the false alarm settlement, as described later, the strikers were enraged; they thought the Forward had left them out in the cold and double-crossed them. The strikers came to the Forward and broke its windows and threatened with destruction until Pine appeared, quieted them and explained that the workers were in error, that it was Rickert and Larger of the United Garment Workers who made the settlement deal and that the Forward group and he were thinking only of the welfare of the strikers. The strikers continued the strike until better terms were obtained.

Pine acted as impartial arbitrator between the Theatre Managers Association and the actors and their union. The managers, Leopold Spachner of the Windsor Theatre, Jacob P. Adler of the Grand Street Theatre, David Kessler of the Thalia Theatre and Boris Tomashefsky of the People's Theatre, were all grateful to Pine for his numerous settlements of disputes between them and their actors.

Maurice Morrison, the great German tragedian, who played in the Windsor Theatre, received the sum of $300.00 per week-end. That was then a high salary. Morrison was of the old school. All was spent by Monday morning. He would appear on Monday mornings and demand from Spachner an advance. Spachner would refuse and berate him for his loose financial habits. Morrison would then counter with "I'm going to send for Max Pine", and the advance was forthcoming. Such was the respect in which Pine was held.

After the tailor strike, Pine again opened a printing shop, this time in the Forward building and continued in the business until 1916, when he again became the Secretary of United Hebrew Trades. Harry Pine ran the business and Max Pine ran about working for others. He was in great demand as a speaker. His name was well advertised on large posters and circulars. He would appear at a meeting hall and note the posters and circulars but noticed also that he did not do the printing work although he was in the printing business and everyone knew it. The fact is that he was a bad business man for himself but a wonderful performer for others.

From 1916 to 1926 he again was the Secretary of the United Hebrew Trades. Upon his retirement from that position he went into the insurance business. When he was asked for an insurance policy, he always tried to keep down the amount so that the insured should not be put to too great a burden to pay the premiums, although that advice seemed to be against his own personal financial interests.

Pine was also the representative of the Jewish Theatrical Alliance and was succeeded by Rubin Guskin, who still held that post until his recent death.

In 1923 he issued the call to organize the Geverkshaften Campaign. In the early part of 1928 Pine, although very sick, left his bed at the Israel Zion Hospital against the advice of the physicians and addressed the Geverkshaften Rally at Cooper Union. This last effort weakened him so that he never recovered from it. Soon after he returned to the hospital, he died. But that was the spirit of Pine: the cause was more important than his own personal well-being.

In "Der Yiddisher Arbeiter" there appears an article by Baruch Zuckerman, dated March 9, 1928, which beautifully characterized Pine as follows:

"His chief characteristic was his warm and pure idealism.

"His life gave the lie to false accusations made by renegades of the American Labor Movement that in America pure idealism is not possible. Pine's forty years of pure idealistic life in America is the best answer.

"A second characteristic was 'fearlessness'. Blessed with a healthy mass instinct that was more sensitive than that of most of the other labor leaders, an instinct which made it possible for him to feel the true characteristics of social changes more quickly than the minds of philosophers with their pure logic could reach, it was that instinct which enabled him to decide upon his course regarding social problems and movements. When he was confronted with a lie, a false line, an empty phrase, no matter how appealing it would be logically, he opposed it, warned others against it and fought it with all his fiery temperament. However, when he felt the truth, a genuineness, a substance, in the social movement—no matter how unpopular the movement might be in his own circle,—he threw himself into the movement with his whole heart and soul, though he stood alone against his comrades, and occasions for such a position were not wanting. To oppose one's own circle is more difficult and requires more courage than opposing the lethargy or inaction of, or unacceptance by, the people of new and untried ideas. In pressing for new ideas one surrounds himself with a group which agrees and gives him moral support. However, to oppose his own circle, one does so with his own personal courage and moral strength and fearlessness.

"Pine was several times tested during his struggle-filled life and was found true.

"His stick-to-it-iveness, courage and fearlessness were most prominently evidenced when he initiated the drive on behalf of Jewish Labor in Palestine. He had to work hard to undo the historic blunder of his comrades, the Bundists, in their opposition to Jewish Labor in Palestine. How he was inflamed by that great injustice perpetrated by the organized Jewish Labor Movement in America upon their brothers in Palestine! How he was overwhelmed by the strong desire to erase the blot from American Jewish Labor with whom and for whom he worked with all his soul! How he raged against his own friends and how happy he was when he heard that one or another of his circle was ready to go along with him!

"His third characteristic was that he was a 'fighter'. That was bound up with his pure idealism and fearless courage. Pine had remarkably powerful weapons. In addition to the normal weapons of strength with which a just cause provides a fighter and ordinary logic to convince others, Pine had his great weapons of folk-humor and folk-satire. He always summoned up an expression, an example, a story, a quotation, a parable, simile, description, which always clinched his point.

"The fourth characteristic was 'kindliness', simple, unadulterated kindliness. He never hurt another; always shared with others his last morsel of bread; had a friendly attitude toward others, and deep love for his friends. He jointly suffered with the oppressed. His heart ached by reason of the poverty and need of others.

"Only a Pine could perform the wonder of organizing immigrants from small towns in East Europe, of different classes, types, who had to break away from their past modes of life and break their moral fibre and backbone. Only Pine's great patience and love for his fellow man could win the respect of the bewildered, fear-stricken, untrusting immigrant.

"Pine was an heroic pioneer. His work in People Relief and Joint Distribution Committee trips to Europe, his reaction to the Friedlander-Cantor episode, American Jewish Congress movement, National Labor Conferences and Congresses—his entire work for the community, was always at his personal material expense and to his personal financial hurt."

In an article in "The Day", a Yiddish daily, of May 29, 1949, A. Epstein sets forth memories of Max Pine. Pine was asked, "What is it that compels you to run to so many meetings? You are not a youngster, you must watch your health, leave the meetings for others, they will do the job. Pine answered: "It isn't that I don't want others to do the job, it is because there is a driving force in me that compels me to go to these meetings and hold speeches before my brother workers."

Pine was blessed with an original speaker's talent. He spoke to his fellow workers with biting humor; he berated them for permitting themselves to be exploited and called them to fight for a better and happier life. The workers loved him because he spoke their language, worked with them in the shops and lived like them.

In addition to his work of organizing and strengthening unions, he toured the country and ceaselessly worked to build the People's Relief Committee. In 1919, he was sent on a mission to bring relief to the Jewish War Sufferers in Poland. In 1921, he was sent to Russia to negotiate with the Bolshevik officials to bring Jewish help to Jewish victims of pogroms in Soviet Russia.

The esteem in which Pine was held by the workers of America can best be illustrated by the number of resolutions of sorrow that arrived at the funeral services. They came from the most important labor unions from Scranton, Rochester, Montreal, Cincinnati, Sioux City, Minneapolis, Chicago, New Bedford, Pittsburgh, Rock Island, Atlanta, Buffalo, Washington, Akron, Philadelphia, Milwaukee, Baltimore, Atlantic City, New Haven, Hartford, Boston, Canton, St. Paul, Providence, San Antonio, Detroit, Malden, and St. Louis.

The esteem in which Pine was held by the people of Palestine, now Israel, can best be illustrated by the fact that a cable of condolence was received from David Ben Gurion, the then leader of labor in Palestine, and now Prime Minister of Israel. An additional illustration is the report of a mass-meeting in Palestine. In the magazine "Kapai Ydiot", of the Palestine Workers' Fund, published in Tel-Aviv, under date of September 3, 1930, there is the following news item:

"A delegation of American leaders of the Geverkshaften consisting of A. Shiplakoff, Chairman of the National Labor Committee for Labor Palestine, M. Feinstone, successor to Pine as Secretary of the United Hebrew Trades, and I. Hamlin, Secretary of the Geverkshaften, toured Palestine. On their arrival in Tel-Aviv on August 20, 1930, a great reception was held at Bet Am where over 7,000 persons gathered to greet them. The stage was bedecked with Red and Blue-White flags. On the walls of the stage hung the portraits of Theodor Herzl, Dov Ber Borochov, A. D. Gordon,

Joseph H. Brenner, Karl Marx and Max Pine. D. Ramaz was the chairman. When he mentioned Pine's name, the entire gathering instinctively rose in a body to pay its respects''.

In ''Der Yiddisher Arbeiter'' under date March 9, there appears an article by Berl Locker, the one time Chairman of the Jewish Agency for Palestine, entitled, ''Max Pine''. There, amongst other things, Locker wrote:

"He was not only a leader, he was like a brother, an integral part of the worker; he was the working class, its destiny, its power.

"He didn't come to the labor movement from the outside, from the Yeshiva, from the university, from the thinkers, from a rich father's table. He grew out of Jewish poverty at a time when the Jewish labor worker was born. He was a part of all the sorrows and griefs that saturated the Jewish worker in America. He suffered through all its defeats and crises of the early years of the movement, not only as a leader, but as a worker and as part of it.

"He never grew away from the working masses. He was deeply rooted in the mother-earth of Jewish labor life and movement.

"His brilliant exhaustless humor streamed from the depths of mass-springs; his social pathos stemmed from the sorrows, feelings and tears of the laboring class.

"He was an organic part of the labor movement. He was one of thousands, but also one of them. The tailor and cloakmaker saw in him a part of himself, an expression of his own potentiality.

"In Pine's rise, the entire Jewish working class saw its own regeneration''.

In the same magazine under date, March 23, 1928, there appears an article by Dov Hoze, the leader of the Histadrut, entitled, "Max Pine" with a sub-title, "The only American Member of the Histadrut." There, amongst other things, Hoze wrote as follows:

"He comes to the ideal of Israel from afar. True, he was always associated with the Jewish worker's life, but he was for many years strange to Palestine. For years the appeal of the Palestinian pioneer found no response in him. For years he could not find even a corner in his great Jewish heart in which there could be engraved that land with its historic meaning, with its new streams of youthful enthusiasm, labor and sacrifices and the hopes that are bound up with it. With his whole heart and soul he was the bearer and fighter of the Jewish worker's interest in America. He carried the yoke of the pioneer and leader in the struggle to create out of newly-arrived immigrants and the masses of self-freed folk. That was sufficient to fulfill his spirit for many years.

"Then suddenly, Max Pine became the first and only American member of the Histadrut. As the voice of building a free, constructive Jewish labor in Palestine at last pierced the closed windows of the American Jewish labor movement, Max Pine became the commander of the new spirit, that of brotherly cooperation between the Jewish worker in America and in Palestine. His young spirit, his close association with our people, his uprightness, his undogmatic view about life's problems, his true anxiety and concern for the future of the Jewish worker, all directed him to the ranks of Palestine labor, disregarding opposition and scorn on all sides. Every worker in Palestine learned that somewhere's very far off, in that great and foreign America, there lives a man, faithful and true, who labors and dreams with us together, who broke down the wall of hate and misunderstanding by our own brother workers in America and who was the first to stretch his hand of brotherhood, the hand of American Jewish labor to the vanguard in Palestine, who took upon itself the difficult, full responsible and full self-sacrificing work in Palestine with such love and devotion.''

Like Moses, it was not Pine's lot to visit Palestine and it was not the good fortune of Palestine to become personally acquainted with him.

Pine died a poor man. He left his wife and four children no material legacy, but he left a great spiritual heritage. His name, by reason of his work, his unstinting devotion to the worker, will be inscribed in history with golden letters. Every struggle, every advancement of the Jewish masses in the United States was the result of his great and untiring work.

Pine's influence on the labor movement and his creation of the bridges between the immigrant and America and between American Labor and Palestine Labor will stand as monuments infinitely superior to any expression of stone, mortar or bronze. His works have increased the well-being of the laboring classes and have helped greatly in the re-creation of a long-suffering people.

Chapter 2

GEVERKSHAFTEN

In the Sunday Forward of February 29, 1948, there appeared the picture of Max Pine with the following inscription:

"Max Pine, unforgettable labor leader—Today, on the 20th Anniversay of his death, he is remembered with reverence as the founder of the Geverkshaften Campaign for Palestine."

Joseph Breslau, Vice-President of the International Ladies Garment Workers' Union, recently wrote about Pine:

"Pine was a brilliant man, with a host of ideas years ahead of his time * * * Max Pine, for example, was years before others in bringing the aims of Labor Palestine to union minds. He stuck to this ideal in the face of stiff left-wing attacks and today, his ideas are part of our accepted program."

The Geverkshaften was a movement which, after a bitter struggle, bound the hundreds of thousands of Jewish Workers in the United States with strong strings of respect and love for the worker in Palestine and to the ideal of Jewish Renaissance in a Jewish State in Palestine, now known as Israel. Pine was the creator of this movement. He saw a vision, thought it through, and then struggled for the realization of that beautiful dream when Jewish Labor, who so opposed a Jewish National rebirth in Palestine, would finally work with heart and soul for such rebirth and devote its money, time, energy and physical and spiritual effort to bring about such rebirth. Pine was the sower of the seeds of such love and devotion for Palestine.

The 26th Annual Conference of the Geverkshaften held at New York in February, 1950, set as its goal the sum of $10,000,000 for Labor Palestine.

Let it be noted that the importance of Pine in his relation to Palestine is not only that he organized the new Geverkshaften as an instrumentality to raise and send millions of dollars to Palestine Labor—that is important enough—but that he and it have caused to be created in the ranks of the masses of American Jewish Labor, where Palestine and Zionism was theretofore taboo, a sympathy and love for the workers in Israel.

Why was there so much opposition in the ranks of American Jewish labor to Zionism and Labor Palestine? To understand the opposition, it is necessary to examine the historical background of the respective movements.

The year 1897 was a memorable year in Jewish History. Modern political Zionism was born with the holding of the First Zionist Congress in Basle, Switzerland. The Basle resolution provided that "Zionism seeks for the Jewish people a publicly recognized, legally secured home in Palestine." The Bund, whose full name was "Algemeinen Yiddisher Arbeiterbund in Litau, Polen and Russland" was also founded that year at a convention in Vilna, Lithuania, then Russia. The Vilna resolution provided that the aims of the Bund were "to fight first and foremost for the improvement of the conditions of the Jewish laborers and for the preaching of Socialism among the Jews.

At first there was no real friction between these two idealistic movements. But in 1901, at its 4th convention at Bialystok, the Bund rejected the idea of political Zionism as a "bourgois reaction to anti-semitism." Thereafter, a bitter struggle developed between the Bund and Zionism for the capture of the heart and mind of the Jew everywhere. This was a struggle between nationalism as translated into Zionism and internationalism as represented by the Bund.

The Bundist Socialists believed that the Jewish people could attain national freedom only through Socialism, and that Jews must remain and struggle for a better world and in whatever land or country they lived, and belong to general socialist groups. Thus only will salvation come to them as well as to all people. World acceptance of Socialism will bring about that salvation.

The Bundist movement spread to the United States and enveloped all the Jewish Labor Socialist leaders here. The Bundist could not make peace with the idea of a Jewish nation or of a Jewish people. He only spoke of the Jewish masses but not of the Jewish people. He refused to talk of Jewish culture but talked of mass culture. He was an opponent of the ideal of Jewish national restoration. He preached that when the world will become truly democratic or socialistic, the plight of the Jew will improve. The Bundist waited for the democratization and socialization of the world and while thus waiting, lost one-third of their brother Jews through Nazi bestiality. He opposed Zionism because it was a nationalistic movement. He argued that, since Socialism advocated the abolition of all nationalism in favor of internationalism, he must fight Zionism. Zionism was not only to be discouraged, ridiculed and mocked at, but also to be fought as well. To the Bundist, Zionism was the big obstacle to his Socialism. The Bundist refused to accept or was ignorant of the works of those philosophic Socialists like Moses Hess, Dr. Nahum Syrkin, Ben Borochov and others, who preached and wrote about the revival of the Jewish Nation on the soil of Palestine based on a cooperative and Socialist society founded on social justice, first propounded by the prophets.

Baruch Zuckerman, then President of the Poale Zion Party in America, —the Socialist-Zionist party, —described the Socialist-Zionist movement as a canvas woven from strings of two live organisms—the Jewish people and the world labor movement. Moses Hess, a co-worker of Karl Marx, wrote "Rome and Jerusalem" in 1862, thus becoming the spiritual founder of the Socialist-Zionist movement and proclaimed the fundamental identity of Judaism's social teaching with the ethics of Socialism; the general labor movement seeks material betterment and spiritual improvement. The Zionist-Socialist movement realized the truths that the Jews were a people like all other peoples and second, that the workers of the world must also call for the national freedom of its people if its people is enslaved. The Zionist-Socialists believed that the Jewish people could obtain its national freedom only through its recreation on its ancestral home, Palestine.

Dr. Nahum Syrkin, a follower of Moses Hess, made popular the gospel of Zionism-Socialism in his German brochure, "The Jewish People and the Socialist Jewish State", published in 1898 under the pseudonym of "Ben Eliezer." It received a great reception. In 1900, Syrkin published his second brochure, "A Call From the Zionist-Socialists to Jewish Youth." He then organized in London the first Zionist-Socialist Society, named, "Forward."

Ben Borochov did likewise in Ekatrineslav, South Russia. In 1909 he was expelled from the Russian Social Democratic Society for "His dangerous influence on worker," due to his Zionist idealism. He then formed the Zionist-Socialist Labor Society.

In Austria, Dr. S. R. Landau published the German monthly, "The Jewish Worker," which propagandized for Jewish renaissance.

In 1899, Jack Behar edited the French monthly, "The Torch" dedicated to Zionism and Socialism.

The Jewish Labor movement in America was at first controlled by the Bundists and was united on behalf of

Jewish Labor in Europe but refused to work for Jewish labor in Palestine.

Pine was one of those Bundist Labor leaders. But, inspired with the ideals of rebuilding Jewish life on productive and Socialist lines wherever there were Jews, he began to disagree with the rest of the Bundists, for to him Palestine became one of those places where Jews lived. And so he determined to do something about breaking the Jewish labor wall of apathy to the idea of a Jewish National Home, or of antagonism to it. In view of his bitter experience with the New York sweat shop, which he helped to abolish, Pine felt more deeply and better understood than the other Bundists the tremendously difficult problems of the new Palestine immigrant who must find a roof over his head, learn a trade, a new language, and accustom himself to his new surroundings in his old-new homeland.

Pine's opportunity came in 1923 and he seized upon it and became the bridge builder between American Jewish Labor and Palestine Labor. He was inspired by the ideologies of self-help, no exploiters, no exploited as practiced in the Socialist Colonies (Kvutsot) in Palestine. To him Socialism had come to life in practice. The organization of the Histadrut in Palestine, laid the foundation for the holy marriage between Palestine Labor and American Jewish Labor with Pine as the Match-maker.

The Histadrut is a unique volunatry labor organization in that it combines trade unions, cooperative, industrial business, immigration, colonization and political activities. Its aim is the creation of a collectivist Jewish Commonwealth and in its ranks are included most of the pioneers and workers in Palestine. It enabled Palestine to receive the large post-war Jewish immigration and to provide employment along the line of ''self-help'' and to care for the cultural and communal needs of immigrants joining it. The Histadrut was a new society where man lived by the labors of his own hands without exploitation of others; a society of no exploiters and no exploited.

Unlike the American Federation of Labor, or the Congress of Industrial Organization, where the worker is only indirectly affiliated with the A. F. of L. and C. I. O. through his membership in a constituent trade union, the membership in the Histadrut is direct. Membership is not confined to members of the trade unions. The members of various labor settlements, cooperative enterprises and collectivist agricultural colonies may also be members of the Histadrut. The Histadrut directs most of the trade unions in Palestine, some of which, by special arrangements, are joint Jewish and Arab unions, with separate branches of each racial group; nearly all collective farms and labor settlements; most cooperative enterprises; operates a vast hospitalization project, the Kupat Cholim, unemployment, old-age, disability and other social security insurance systems, a workers' bank, an educational system, the largest cooperative construction company, Solel Boneh, a sports' organization, a theatre, immigration and colonization departments, and before the establishment of Israel, a militia, the Haganah.

The Histadrut captured the imagination of Max Pine. He saw his idealism put into practice in the land of Israel. He had spirit, courage and boldness to fight for his convictions with a great heart that bled for Jewish suffering and the sorry plight of the Jewish people everywhere, including Palestine.

At first, he was practically alone among the American Jewish labor leaders. But soon he convinced enough of them to follow him and in August, 1923, he called together a group of Jewish labor leaders and organized the "National Labor Committee for Organized Jewish Labor in Palestine." Since Pine was then Secretary and Executive Director of the United Hebrew Trades known in Yiddish as the "Geverkshaften", he was able to obtain the permission of

U. H. T. to use the name of "Geverskshaften" for the National Labor Committee for Palestine, which he then created. Ossip Walinsky of the Pocket Book Workers' Union presided at that organizational meeting. Pine was elected Chairman of the compaign committee. The quota adopted was $150,000.

Pine's first task was to form a representative committee of labor leaders in behalf of his cause. The road was thorny and difficult, for most leaders refused to be associated with him in the drive. However, a number of courageous labor leaders did place themselves under Pine's direction; amongst them that unforgettable tribune, Abraham Shiplakoff, who succeeded Pine as leader upon Pine's death; J. Goldstein of the Bakers' Union; Max Zuckerman of the Cap Workers' Union; Morris Feinstone, the successor to Shiplakoff after his death; Joseph Schlossberg and Jacob Potofky of the Amalgamated Clothing Workers; Baruch Zuckerman; Harry Lang of the Forward; Israel Feinberg of the I. L. G. W. U.; Alexander Kahn, lawyer, Max Zaritsky, I. H. Goldberg and Alex Rose of the Millinery Union; A. Liesin, poet, H. Rogoff, Newspaperman, Ossip Walinsky; M. G. Wolpert and others.

After forming his committee, Pine arranged for the First Geverkshaften Campaign Mass Meeting on February 13, 1924, at Cooper Union Auditorium. He opened the meeting with his maiden speech for Palestine:

> "This is an enormously important get-to-gether because tonight we open our campaign for $150,000 for Jewish Labor in Palestine and we will not rest until we are completely successful.

> "Since this campaign will be national in scope, it is necessary that the impress and influence of this meeting shall be spread far and wide in every corner of Jewish labor in America, in every

shop, in every community where Jewish labor resides.

"This meeting is even more important because of a great historic event. This is the first time that Jewish workers in America meet to destroy a dogma and throw off the shackles that kept in chains thousands of our sisters and brothers whom destiny has brought to Palestine.

"In addition I might add that this meeting is highly significant by reason of the moral prestige which will be added to Jewish Labor in Palestine because this is the first occasion of its recognition by Jewish Labor in America.

"They need our recognition desperately because the Histadrut, being a class organization, a workers' organization which struggles for the economic and political improvement of the thousands of workers, will, through our recognition, receive additional strength and courage.

"What is it that created this campaign and this interest in our brothers in Palestine?

"Several months ago the Histadrut wrote a letter to the U. H. T., a part of which is the following:

"The Jewish Labor movement in Palestine is now 18 years old. It grew and developed through Jewish immigration which became particularly heavy when, after the World War, despite all obstacles, 35,000 came to Palestine between 1919 and 1923.

"The immigrants are either workers or work-seeking elements, employables. Histadrut became an organization of 17,000 registered workers in 100 communities. Before the war there were only 2,700 registered workers there.

"In that letter they describe their great difficulties in getting accustomed to agricultural and industrial work in a backward country, where they were confronted with the problems of ignorant and unorganized workers.

"They also state that to this general Jewish Workers' Organization (Histadrut) belong workers of different backgrounds and parties, and others without party affiliation. They organized there their industrial, cultural and agricultural institutions on a very modern order. As a labor organization, it is of a higher form than our own, for they are a part of the organized world labor movement.

"In their letter, they ask us to send them a delegation which shall acquaint itself with their work on the spot, with their urban and land cooperative undertakings, so that they could acquaint American Jewish Labor with them, their accomplishments and their needs and then see what it can do to increase the scope and opportunities of a large labor immigration into Palestine.

"Our labor movement declined a delegation for a reason not necessary here to discuss. However, I was assured that there are enough Jewish workers here ready to help the workers in Palestine. Upon this ground we, labor leaders in America, organized this campaign with the promise to make it a great success.

"Therefore, we called together this meeting to inaugurate our campaign for $150,000 for Jewish Labor in Palestine.

"Who are these Jewish workers in Palestine? They were recruited from the blooming youth, who, saturated with idealism, enthused with a mystic love for their unfortunate people, set out for Palestine, carrying in their hearts a great and shining hope that they are going to create a home for their brothers and sisters who were drowning in blood and in tears and who survived all misfor-tunes and catastrophies.'' (This was stated ten years before Hitler came to power.)

''These children of Israel, many of whom never knew economic need, coming into a land about which they dreamed so sweetly, and which the Bible described as beautiful, were met face to face with the hard, cruel reality. They met the test. They broke the rocks with the most primitive instruments, tilled the long neglected soil, suffered from the Eastern Sun, at times without water to satisfy their thirst, and without bread, and were attacked by disease and unfriendly Arabs. Their lives were always in danger. Despite these ob-stacles, they stubbornly carried on and perma-nently settled on the soil.

''They created institutions that are not only an honor for themselves but also a credit for the workers of the world. Their trade union move-ment, their produce and consumer cooperatives carry the stamp of true workers' unity. This caused us to recognize their struggle and accept them as our own brothers. They are making great efforts to broaden their activities not only for their own improvement, but also to enable new im-migrants to come and be absorbed in the economy of the country. They know that the greater the Jewish population in Palestine will be, the more the country will develope and the easier will be the lot of those living there.

''Therefore, the workers of Palestine do all they can for the new immigrants. They divide their work, they cut off a piece of their own meager bread to give it to the tired immigrants.

"Because of the tragic situation in Europe, because they have little exports, and because of other hard economic situations, the workers are living through a crisis in Palestine and we must help them overcome it. We must help support their institutions and enable them to bring into their country thousands of new immigrants, who are wanderers in all the eastern countries without hope to settle in some peaceful corner.

"Let us not confuse the help that we, Jewish labor of America through the People's Relief, gave to the workers of all other countries. When representatives of Labor institutions came to us from Warsau and Chernowitz, we did not send them to the People's Relief, but we carried out separate special campaigns for those institutions. Such institutions are more important in Palestine than in the other countries. Palestine is the only country in the world outside of America that can show such substantial immigration of our Jewish employables. Our campaign is not to send charity to the workers that are already in Palestine. We determine with them to help thousands of immigrants to come into the land. It is, therefore, unjust to count the number of Jews there and to distribute this 'thinned-soup help' so that each could get a plate of soup.

"There are amongst us those who fear that perhaps our campaign would give new courage to Zionists. These are still afraid that Jews are making a bad 'bargain' with Zion. I ask: 'Why should I fear them more than Ramsey MacDonald, than Snowden, Wedgwood and others? If they have no fear, why should I fear?'

"No, Jewish Labor here will not get frightened by such arguments. American Jewish Labor which has so distinguished itself by its deeds, assisting all labor and social undertakings, will, in this campaign exhibit even greater will, interest and energy, always with the thought that the money will bring greater uses, for with this money there will be purchased tools, there will be built institutions that will be as beacon lights that will brighten and beautify the life of the workers in Palestine and make it possible for them to make room and create work for new immigrants.

"All that we own, all our spirit, all our energy must be thrown into this campaign.

"And when this campaign will be concluded, and Palestine Jewish Labor will see that they are not alone in their difficulties, their hearts will be filled with joy and hope for a better, brighter future for themselves and for the entire working class."

It is interesting to note that that speech was made by a man who was never a member of the Zionist movement, was not even a member of Poale-Zion, the Socialist-Zionist party.

It is also important to note that labor leaders were not the only ones afraid of the idea of Zionism. Even the highly idealistic persons who were in control of the Jewish Publication Society—the upper strata of Jewish life in America—also were in the beginning opposed to Zionism. Henrietta Szold, who later became the founder and leader of Hadassah, the Women's Zionist Organization— then the Secretary of the literary committee of the Jewish Publication Society, wrote Dr. Stephen S. Wise on March 26, 1899, that the Society would not print a book on Zionism. Her words were—"The publication of Zionist literature by the Jewish Publication Society, I can say with almost perfect confidence, that the proposition would not be met with favor. * * *

"The Society cannot risk a book on Zionism."

This, in spite of the fact that she then believed that Zionism was a movement of the greatest magnitude and "the only real movement in Judaism today."

It is to be noted that since then the Jewish Publication Society has printed many leading Zionist books.

Pine then issued his first campaign call in March, 1924, which reads as follows:

"Dear Friend,

You have undoubtedly heard that the U. H. T. of New York, Chicago and Philadelphia, in collaboration with many leaders of organized Jewish Labor, undertook to raise a fund of $150,000 for the Jewish Workers in Palestine.

"As Chairman of the National Campaign Committee, I take the liberty of appealing to you to aid in this drive and to enable us, not only to raise the amount set, but to go over the top and oversubscribe it.

"This is our first constructive relief effort for the Jewish workers of Palestine; our first attempt to render them financial and moral support. The money raised will be forwarded to them for tools and machinery and for the improvement of their institutions.

"The launching of this camapign, which is in fact our first recognition of labor in Palestine, required an enormous amount of time, courage and work. Those of us who organized and are conducting this drive are giving freely of our money, energy and best efforts for the workers of Palestine.

"WHAT WILL YOU CONTRIBUTE TOWARDS THIS
NOBLE CAUSE?

"Let your immediate response and your hearty
cooperation enable us to achieve our goal and to
wind up this campaign with the greatest success.

"Expecting to hear from you, I remain,

Sincerely yours,

Max Pine, Chairman."

Pine threw himself into the campaign with his whole
heart and soul. He traveled throughout the country,
visited and spoke to most of the 60 communities in 20
states of the United States and three cities of Canada,
where local committees were formed to help. $51,165.96
was raised and the first remittance to Palestine was made
on June 26, 1924.

The Histadrut acknowledgment of the first remittance
contained the following:

"Your opening campaign has aroused tremendous hopes in the ranks of labor in this country.
When Jewish labor of the world will be united and
will have understanding and sympathy for our
cause, only then will be found our national partners and there will then be created the true spirit
and strength with which we will overcome all obstacles. Your first remittance was an indication
that such time is approaching and especially now,
when in our established Palestine labor positions,
opponents are arising on all sides; your work is
doubly comforting. Your activity not only brought
us funds, but it brought us strengthened courage
and hope."

Upon receipt of the *Reply of the Histadrut,* Max Pine issued the following proclamation, and printed it in The Forward:

"We know no better way to inform our friends regarding the results of the recently concluded campaign which the U. H. T. together with important Jewish labor organizations carried on for the Organization of Jewish Labor in Palestine, than to publicize this remarkable document which was sent us from the Histadrut of Palestine.

"We are certain that with us all those who helped in the campaign either as workers or givers will be proud and happy.

"We do not wish to convince ourselves that the campaign was a high success. When we compare our campaign with others that were carried on at the same time by other organizations, for other purposes, we have good reason for being satisfied. But we refuse to make such comparisons. We, of course, know that there is a very strong spirit among our American workers on behalf of Jewish Labor in Palestine. Were we capable to make full use of this spirit, the results would have been much greater. The Campaign Committee, of which I have the honor to be chairman, does not regard this as its last campaign. We will yet come before the Jewish Masses and demand of them to fulfill the duty they owe to Jewish Labor in Palestine, for the heroic efforts they make under such trying conditions, a work which is of great meaning for the entire Jewish people in general and for the Jewish laboring classes throughout the world in particular.

"It is for that reason that we do not now draw up our totals for the campaign for we want all who helped us to become acquainted with the message of Palestine so that all may know the purposes for which the monies were used.

"We hope that all who receive this brochure will read the entire message. Read every word of it and ask yourself if there exists elsewhere in the entire world organized Jewish Labor which through its very existence builds the foundations for freedom as well as Socialism for an entire people? Ask yourself whether you know of another place where the processes of creating Jewish life is so courageously carried on with such collossal success and direct through Jewish Labor? Ask yourself whether you know of another land in the world where such a large group of Jewish workers established for itself such a sound, strong, economic position as Jewish Labor in Palestine? Do you know of any other land where labor has been raised to such a lofty position as in the new Jewish life in Palestine? Did anyone hear of any higher or finer example of self-sacrifice for the benefit of the community?

"Read it all! Hide it in the recesses of your memory! And when we come to you a second time, let us find you a friendly co-worker. May our work of the past campaign not be wasted.

"With brotherly love and in the name of the Geverkshaften Campaign Committee,

Max Pine, Chairman."

Pine had faith in the basic fairness and justice of the common man. He was a true democrat. While he was being ridiculed by the leaders of labor who opposed the whole idea of the Geverkshaften campaign, he always had faith in the union members themselves.

In the early days of the campaign, during those bitter days of socialist opposition, Pine said to Meyer Castoff, a delegate to the U. H. T. from the Typesetters Union, "Don't worry, you'll see that the masses will sooner or later come to us. They must come. With those leaders that do not yet understand our truths or refuse to understand us, we should not fight. We should rather turn our gaze to our friends, the workers of our unions. How willing and ready they are to help. Let us rather carry on our practical work and victory will of necessity be ours in due time."

He was right. In the 1949 campaign, almost $5,000,000 was raised and the entire Jewish and non-Jewish labor movement was behind the Geverkshaften Campaign. How the unions and workers threw themselves into the work of helping Histadrut in the great historic struggle for a Jewish Homeland! It must be observed that what the Poale-Zion—the Socialist-Zionist Party which was founded in 1903—could not do, bring American labor to the Zionist ideal, —Pine and the Geverkshaften founded 20 years later, did.

In November 1925, Pine called a labor conference to organize the Second Geverkshaften Campaign. Three hundred delegates representing 158 labor organizations met at the first organization meeting held at the Hias Building on January 2, 1926. Colonel Josiah Wedgewood, vice-President of the British Labor Party, one of the leading non-Jewish Zionist sympathizers, was the principal speaker. He added greatly to the spirit of the occasion. A quota of one-quarter million dollars was adopted. The Geverkshaften was thereupon declared a permanent body. The first mass meeting of the second campaign was held at Cooper Union on January 14, 1926, attended by Yitzhak Ben Zvi, now president of Israel, David Ramaz and Joseph Baratz, Histadrut delegates from Palestine. A collection was made at that meeting and $40,000 was raised in cash and pledges.

Then the campaign gained momentum with meetings in Boston, Philadelphia, Chicago, Cleveland, Winnipeg, Toronto, Montreal, Detroit, Pittsburgh, Newark, New Haven, Hartford, Los Angeles and other communities. Pine addressed most of these meetings. Committees were organized in 100 cities in 25 states and in Canada. The Committee also carried out intensive propaganda for the cause. At the Manhattan Opera House meeting on April 3, there were 3,000 in the audience. Chaim Nachman Bialik, the greatest modern Hebrew poet, was the principal speaker.

One Hundred Thirteen Thousand dollars was raised from 15,000 contributors. This showed the mass response to the appeal. Of said sum, $87,476.74 in cash or in kind was sent to Palestine. The balance of approximately $25,000 was used for campaign expenses. While that sum seems large—expenses of 29% of income—in fact it is a rather low figure for expenses, since the movement was comparatively new and a great deal of propaganda and expenses was needed to break through the wall of Socialist opposition to the campaign. It is also to be noted that the said sum included expenses for the Histadrut delegation from Palestine. (The three mentioned above were joined later by Benjamin Hartzfeld).

To show the variety of Palestine organizations and activities that was helped by the Geverkshaften, the following report of Isaac Hamlin, the Secretary, is enlightening:

To Solel Bonch—construction cooperative ... $25,620.00

For cultural activities (kindergarten, schools, youth clubs, libraries, etc.) 13,340.00

To Palestine Labor Fund 9,765.00

To Histadrut for general expenses 8,392.71

For organization of trade unions 7,420.00

To Kupat Cholim (Clinics, hospitals, sanitaria) 7,150.00

Land Coops 3,740.00

To build a Labor Lyceum 2,500.00

Women's Groups 2,295.00

Urban Industrial Coops. 1,535.00

Immigration Committee of Histadrut........ 500.00

Sent tools, machines and exhibits of the value of 5,219.03

Total accounted for...... $87,476.74

At a meeting of the Geverkshaften Committee on July 8, 1926, a resolution was adopted to send to Palestine a delegation consisting of Pine, Schlossberg and Shiplakoff. Unfortunately, Pine became ill and could not go.

The second Geverkshaften Campaign proved that Pine was not a dreamer but a practical worker for his cause. In order to overcome the strong Socialist opposition to his campaign he planned to win the sympathy of Abraham Cahan, the leading Jewish Socialist. He made arrangements for Cahan to visit Palestine and see with his own eyes the miracle that was being performed by the Histadrut.

One evening Pine was sitting in Scholom's Cafe on Division Street with Dr. Mordecai Katz and Professor Getsel Zelikowitz. They were discussing the worker in Palestine. Pine suddenly observed that he would soon be able to broaden the work of the Geverkshaften Campaign on a large scale and all unions, even the Socialist organizations—who then opposed him bitterly—would take part. The wise professor winked to the doctor, as one would say: "This Pine is off the beam, he is a dreamer and dreams a sweet dream." Everyone knew that Cahan and the Forward crowd, to be kind to them, were not enthusiastic about the Geverkshaften Campaign—the official sanction or approval had not yet been forthcoming. Pine caught the wink, understood and said: "Soon Abe Cahan will visit Palestine. I wrote to the Jewish leaders there to give him a hearty welcome, as if he were a friend, and to show him the great achievements of the chalutzim, and the important work of the Jewish idealists in Palestine. You will see, when Cahan will return, he and the Forward will help the Geverkshaften Campaign and the work will be broadened in all Jewish unions and Socialist organizations." And so it was.

Cahan's opposition to the Zionist ideal can best be illustrated by his report in the Forward of the First Zionist Congress held at Basle in 1897. One can realize the resistance that the concept of Jewish national rebirth encountered among the Socialists and laboring classes of America by noting those headlines. The Forward of August 30, 1897 under the editorship of Cahan carried the following headline: "Dr. Herzl 'Der Nayer Moshe,' (translated— The New Moses) with the news item dated Basle, August 30, 1897, Basle, Switzerland: "Just a trifling—a complete tiny trifling—that is the object of Dr. Herzl and his Jewish Nationalists to take Jews out of the Galut and bring them to a land where worms eat the people not only after death but during their very lives."

The September 1, 1897 Forward headline reads: "Bomb number three" "Fifty million dollars—"That is all that Dr. Herzl needs to become the Messiah."

It was such derision which continued up to the last days of Pine. By proper planning Pine eventually overcame Cahan's opposition and turned him into a sympathizer at the Third Geverkshaften Campaign.

The Third Annual Geverkshaften Campaign Convention for organized Jewish Labor in Palestine was held at the Forward Hall on January 2, 1927. The convention was attended by 452 delegations from 174 organizations as follows:

10 Central Labor Organizations	40	delegates
28 City Community Committees	66	"
2 Independent Workmen's Circle Branches	6	"
30 Jewish National Workers' Alliance Branches	78	"
24 Unions	64	"
26 Workmen's Circle Branches	68	"
22 Poale—Zion Societies	61	"
16 Young Zionist groups	37	"
11 Women's Clubs	18	"
1 Leather Cooperative	2	"
4 Left Poale-Zion groups	12	"

Pine was again unanimously elected the national chairman and he received a tremendous ovation. When the ovation was concluded, Pine remarked:

"Many are satisfied with the results of the last campaign. The chairman himself is not. It is true that we raised twice the sum we raised in the first campaign. But that is not the test.

"Taking into account the number of persons who participated in the campaign and the effort and energy put into the work, the sum raised was not large. I say this not in beautiful words and phrases but in the most seriousness and earnestness at my command. I repeat—that to raise $113,000 after such hard labor is not sufficient for me. Our income was not in $10,000 donations; it was derived from quarters, dollars, fives and tens, twenty-fives and a few hundreds. And so much work and time was needed to collect it. I know all this. Despite all this effort, I say we did not raise sufficient funds, particularly with relation to the great undertaking for which the money was being raised.

"Just think, the recent strike of 8 bakers cost $70,000; the cloakmakers' strike cost $4,000,000. Then compare the sum we collected with the needs of Palestine institutions and you will see the inadequacy of our collection.

"The situation in Palestine is not rosy. Show me a land in Europe, particularly a small land, which is not in urgent need. Palestine just got on its feet. They just built institutions which need support. They keep them up as best they can, but they cannot expand their activities. Brother Arlasaroff explained to me that in Petach Tikvah the 2,000 workers wanted the Hamashbir (consumer co-op), which has branches in all important sections of Palestine, to establish a branch there. But Hamashbir decided not to establish it at Petach Tikva for lack of funds. Every dollar you sent there builds and develops. *If there were no other reason than to deny the falsehood that Jews are not capable of working and building, for this alone, our work would have been worth while.*

"Two years ago we organized 60 committees, now we have committees in 100 cities. I am certain that with our will and determination we will raise one-quarter million dollars this year. I assure you that even the few opponents that are still here will never again oppose a yearly campaign.

"In Hamlin's financial report there is included the Histadrut report of their disbursements of the monies we sent them. Every cent we sent them went to support a worthy and particular institution to build, create, enlarge its position and enable Jewish Labor in Palestine to receive not only encouragement but also a place to establish itself.

"I hope we will make great efforts to make the campaign a great success. I greet all delegates, particularly those that have come from out-of-town. I greet you all, brothers and sisters, who are united in this holy cause and who will work until our brothers and sisters in Palestine will no longer need our help." (Loud and long applause)

Dr. Chaim Arlasaroff, member of the Executive of Histadrut, a visitor from Israel, was the principal speaker who said, among other things:

"It is an historic work to bring to the attention of American Jewish labor masses the great ideal of our national and social freedom for which Palestine Jewish labor stands. In its early beginnings Jewish Labor in Palestine was scoffed and laughed at; we were considered as romantic dreamers; they expressed it that we dreamed of a Jerusalem in heaven while we spoke of Jerusalem on earth; created a land not of heaven but of earth. The dream of a "One Big Union" was realized in

Palestine through Histadrut. Histadrut is a trade union organization which also has other functions. It also is a mighty power of colonization in Palestine. We have created the first all Jewish city in Palestine—Tel Aviv—and organized its administrative and legislative functions. Jewish labor thirsts for a new life and to create life.

"We are united not only for the attainment of our inspirational goal, but perhaps as a result of our united effort, we may create among the greatest social constructive values in the whole world."

WILLIAM GREEN, President of the A. F. of L. sent the following greeting to the meeting: "Wishing you and all your associates all possible success in your campaign to raise funds for organized labor in Palestine."

ABRAHAM CAHAN, Editor of The Forward, was then introduced. He said he traveled through the Kvutzot; till then he was unfamiliar with their accomplishments. But, after seeing and speaking to those idealists, he was convinced that it would be a disgrace if the Americans did not help them.

He then said: "I remained neutral in the struggle between the Bund and Poale Zion. After seeing Ain Harod, Tel Joseph, the cities, etc., I felt that to be intolerant to those idealists would be a crime."

He said he was not interested with disputes in Warsaw between the parties or what his Socialist friends here would think of him, and if they are not happy with him for he does not agree with them. He then continued:

"I tell them I came from a land where the people are different and Marxism is a theory of circumstances.

"I join with you to help Histadrut. I see no reason why Socialists should combat Poale-Zion.

"I am not a Zionist in the accepted term, but I sympathize with them. Together we can go far. I will do all in my power to help Palestine Labor, to lighten its burden. They hunger too much and work too hard and have too little sunshine in their lives except for their spiritual sunshine.

"One must be a murderer to see those noble souls, how they work, and not sympathize and help them. I feel that these theories and policies of Socialist tolerance will help us here in America. I am certain that when all will know what the Histadrut is and does, all will join the conference. I wish the conference great success." (Enthusiastic applause)

A. Revutsky offered a resolution that the funds raised should go solely for economic institutions and not for cultural institutions. Max Pine opposed it and it was defeated 203 to 33. Max Zuckerman was reelected Treasurer, and Isaac Hamlin, Secretary. The quota adopted was $250,000.

As a result of the January 2 meeting, Pine issued the following call to the 3rd Annual Geverkshaften Campaign:

"To You Jewish Workers of America

"Dear Brothers and Friends:

"Again our brothers, Organized Jewish Labor in Palestine, has issued a call from their fields and forests, the villages and towns. They ask greater means for the broadening of their work, for the establishment of new positions, for more and more immigrant wanderers in the old-new homeland.

"The Histadrut, the organization which represents these workers in the institutions in Palestine, is a wonderful labor organization. There is no such second organization in the world that is so exemplary in its conduct and in achievement, and in the self-sacrifice and heroism of its leaders and members.

"This organization turns to us, to the workers of America.

"And we, a large number of our responsible labor organizations and labor leaders of America now issue the third call for a campaign to raise ¼ million dollars for workers' and Socialist institutions in Palestine.

"We, therefore, appeal to the laboring masses and all who sympathize with them, to join in the great and historic work, in order to make our campaign a great success.

"In our last campaign we raised $113,000. We are certain that this year we will double the sum.

"A successful campaign will demonstrate to our brothers and sisters in Palestine that their work, achievements and sacrifice have touched the depths of our hearts, that we hold high and appreciate the sacrifices they bring in order to give courage to the unfortunates of our people and to bring honor to the labor movement everywhere.

"Our work hasn't the appearance of charity. It is not a matter of immediate relief. Our effort is to help build, build new and enlarge existing institutions so that our brothers and sisters there will be enabled to live productive lives and make more room for new immigrants, new Jewish homeless wanderers without legal rights who can find in the entire great world no other place to rest.

"It is true that times are not good for immigrants in Palestine. That is because all of Europe is going through a crisis which is reflected in the entire Near East. But these workers did not go to Palestine to make money and then run from there. They came to settle there permanently. That is their land and will remain their land for their children.

"There, therefore, devolves upon us a holy duty —as workers and as Jews—to stand beside them in their difficult time, to help them achieve a more beautiful and successful life so that they will no longer need our material help.

"We again call upon our brothers and sisters to again make their contributions in money and in work, to make it possible to raise one-quarter million dollars.

"The time for philosophizing and argumentation about our rights to sympathize with Palestine Labor is past. If, by this time we have not yet convinced our opponents of our just cause, it would be a waste of time and energy to try it again.

"The time for work has arrived. Each one who wants to help should lend a brotherly hand. We need not apologize for our work, we are proud of it.

"When we enter upon our campaign we take full cognizance of the sacrifice made by Palestine labor for their ideals. They shed their blood there. They carried on a fight not only against unfriendly and aroused enemies, but also against the bitter and deadly living elements of nature, against fever, hunger, thirst. They never for a moment quit their work for they believed in their ideals and undertakings, for they see the end of their difficult road. They see that their heroic efforts will soon be turned into credits—the trust, faith and wonder of organized labor throughout the world.

"Let us begin and end our 3rd Campaign with the same determination, the same courage, with but a one-thousandth part of their self-sacrifice, and we will have the greatest success.

"To work, brothers and sisters! You who work in the factories and shops in this blessed, developed land, put your shoulder to the wheel and help Jewish Labor in Palestine create one strong labor position after another, help them develop a productive, social and cultural life; help them save more and more Jewish unemployed from the economic ruin of East Europe.

"With true brotherly greetings to all our friends and to the large army of our co-workers, I remain,

> Max Pine, Chairman of the
> National Labor Committee
> for Organized Jewish Labor
> in Palestine.

Endorsed by the United Hebrew Trades

Send your checks and contributions to our National Treasurer, Max Zuckerman, Treasurer, Palestine Labor Campaign, 32 Union Square, N.Y. N.Y."

Pine threw himself into the third Campaign with the full fire of his soul. He campaigned at such a pace as to weaken himself physically. The campaign succeeded. At the end of 1927, he was taken to the Israel-Zion Hospital where he was bedridden.

Plans for the fourth Geverkshaften Campaign were being made without him, for he was not be disturbed. However, through "The Forward", he learned of the opening mass meeting to be held at Cooper Union on January 1, 1928 in the form of a reception to the Histadrut delegation. Pine left his bed and appeared at the mass meeting.

He was introduced, received an ovation, delivered his farewell speech; returned to the hospital, and died two months later.

Pine spoke as follows:

"With a feeling of real joy I proclaim in the name of all our co-workers, that we are proud of our accomplishments in 1927.

"We thought that last year was a year of crisis and we were truly worried. But the great work of the last delegation, the great effort of all our friends everywhere and our great faith in the nobility of our cause, all of this not only brought about a financial success, but also added to our ranks, persons and organizations that are an honor for the movement.

"And what do we expect in 1928? As for ourselves, I expect that when we will gather again next year, we shall be surprised at our great results.

"However, we should not believe that things will be easier because our opposition do not let us alone and will continue to oppose us in the future. The fact is that for months there has been going on an underground propaganda against us and we cannot even answer the opposition because it is cowardly and underground. However, in spite, of this the new drive will be most successful and fruitful.

"This year's campaign must open up the hearts of the masses. In addition to making a heart-rending appeal, we shall likewise issue loud protests which shall be as stormy as the sea in its unrest. They shall be so great as to fully express the woe and sorrow of those striving for their freedom.

"Against whom will we protest? First, against those who should be with us and are not. Second; against a large section of the leaders of the Zionist Organization of America; Third, against a section of the leadership of the World Zionist Organization who abandoned the Palestine Chalutz in his critical plight and did not sufficiently concern itself with putting an end to unemployment.

"A large number of Jewish Socialists accuse me that I do not follow party discipline by reason of my participation in these campaigns. I proclaim that this accusation is not true. I maintain that it is they who break party discipline by their refusal to help us and continue in their slander and undercover opposition tactics against us. International Socialism has already recognized the worker in Palestine as a part of the world labor movement. Therefore, every Socialist who works against the interests of the workers in Palestine is rebelling against the resolutions and principles of International Socialism. He is the breaker of party discipline.

"With regard to the matter of discipline in the American Socialist Party, we have its official recognition in the form of a letter which Eugene V. Debs addressed to our 1926 Geverkshaften Campaign conference at Chicago in which he wished our undertaking great success, expressing his regrets that he could not be with us personally due to his health. Besides, the National Executive of the Socialist Party sent us Prof. George Kilpatrick, its Secretary, who brought personal greetings in its behalf.

"If this isn't sufficient proof to establish the fact that we are correct in our dealings and true to our principles. then in order to satisfy our critics we should don sacks, cover our heads with ashes and ask for forgiveness of them who hold themselves greater than Og, the king of Bashan and haven't sufficient courage to attack us openly.

"We protest against those who should be with us and are not and who carry on an underground war against us.

"We shall make a powerful protest against those World Zionist leaders who should know, better than all, the role of Jewish Labor in Palestine and the enormous sacrifices the workers have been making there and who still did not have sufficient courage to resist the rich American uncle who has only to his credit a fat bank-book.

"We shall make a powerful protest against most of the leaders of American Zionism who compelled the World Zionist Congress at Basle to cut $\frac{1}{2}$ of the budget for workers' institutions in Palestine in the face of that terrible crisis, thus endangering their great economic and cultural institutions. They have thus clearly demonstrated that they desire to break the power of the workers and to lower their prestige and weaken the courage of their heroic overworked leaders. At all their conventions they constantly repeat how much Palestine has cost them. They refuse to recognize for one moment that for every dollar they contributed, the worker of Palestine has contributed one quart of blood. No one has yet died from any contribution to the Keren Hayesod or Keren Kayemet. Those, however, who dried the swamps, left long rows of graves in which are interred the finest and best children of our people. Because of all of this and because of the serious situation in Palestine, we must gird our loins and make the strongest exertion on behalf of our coming campaign.

"A large collection will show the world that the Chalutz is not a friendless orphan; it will show that he has a brother in America who is ready to protect him. At our conferences, in the voices of our speakers, there must be clearly bared the heavy laden soul of the workers of Palestine, there must be clearly heard the cry of the children of the unemployed, the still cry of their mothers, and at the same time the awakened voice of the workers who build, create and are certain of their goal. Our speakers must convey to the audiences the great responsibility that is ours towards Palestine Labor now more than ever before. We must insist that the large number of workers who will get funds from others, should set the example and themselves give.

"Jewish workers were arrested in Petach Tikva because they resisted attempts to relieve them of their work. I can't believe that the attack and arrest by the police was an accident. I am certain that the attack was made because of the manner in which the workers were treated by the World Zionist leaders and the Congress at Basle.

"We are certain that with our help the Histadrut will put an end to the crisis. Just as they were able to reduce unemployment by half, they will be able to put an end to it completely. We are certain that with the sincere devotion, with the exemplary self-sacrifice of the leaders of the Histadrut and its 36,000 members, together with the moral and financial help which we will provide, the Histadrut will succeed to open the gates of Palestine to the tens of thousands of Jewish Chalutzim in East Europe who are impatiently waiting to go there to begin to establish for themselves a life of productive labor.

"Let us with great enthusiasm set out to do the job. May our campaign be a great success. Let our quota of $300,000 be oversubscribed."

The Geverskshaften Campaign went from strength to strength. It converted millions of non-believers and disbelievers to the cause of Labor Palestine. The entire American Labor movement, the American Federation of Labor under William Green and since his death on November 21, 1952, under George Meany, also the Committee of Industrial Organization under Philip Murray and since his death on November 9th, 1952, under Walter Reuther, assisted and are affiliated with the movement for Labor Palestine and with Zionist affairs generally. All four presidents, Green, Murray, Reuther and Meany never refused to intervene on behalf of Jewish Palestine and Israel whenever necessary. Green and Murray saw the President on the matter of British arming of the Arabs. Even David Dubinsky, President of the I. L. G. W. U., a former antagonist, is now standing at the behest and service of Jewish Labor in Israel.

The Geverkshaften has continued to spread information about Palestine and Israel and stimulated enthusiasm for the Jewish Homeland.

It has brought home to the American public that Histadrut regards the Arab masses as brothers of Jewish Labor and is seeking to lift their standard of living so that the two peoples could live side by side in civilized peace, harmony, equality and enjoy the benefits of democracy and contentment.

In summation, it must be acknowledged that the establishment of Israel as a sovereign state and its acceptance by the United Nations has proven the bankruptcy of the ideas of the Bundists. They based their ideology on a non-existent proletarian world. Internationalism necessarily had to liquidate itself for it was a mirage. There are today national Socialist parties in democratic lands and national communist parties in the lands of the Soviet bloc. Both Socialism and Communism are now nationalistic and territorialistic and not internationalistic.

It was Pine who saw the changed circumstances many year ago and preached it even against strong opposition. Pine's views were proved to be correct.

Though Pine never visited Palestine, his name and his works have become household expressions there. To honor his memory, the Histadrut established in 1929, the Max Pine Trade School in Tel-Aviv, as a training center for fitters, mechanics and electricians, where 3,000 students attended in 1950 and more today.

Chapter 3

THE TAILOR STRIKE

Judge Jacob Panken, of the Domestic Relations Court of the City of New York and former law partner of Judge Morris Rothenberg, an ex-president of the Zionist Organization of America and of the Jewish National Fund of America and whose son, Nathaniel S. Rothenberg, is the present nassi-president of Bnai Zion, in discussing the qualities, character and personality of Max Pine, said the following:

"He was always ready and willing to do something for some one, even for his ideological opponent. He helped countless people. This set him apart from others of his group in the esteem of the masses of the working class. His thoughts were not only for the individual Jewish worker, but also for mankind in general. He was part of the movement and press of Jewish radicalism. He was not a Zionist and never belonged to any Zionist group, not even the Poale Zion. He was, however, a Jewish nationalist and Jewish cultural heritage was constantly in his soul and his mind's eye.

"Upon his arrival here, he started to have impact upon the freethinker to return to his ageless Jewish culture. He preached interest in its spiritual treasures. He insisted upon a wedding between Jewish nationalism and socialism so as to become equal partners.

"He was a devotee of Jewish national culture. He was not an orator, he was a logician. He was very human. He loved to live and lived to love the laboring masses in general and the Jewish laboring masses in America and in Palestine in particular.

"He was a cultured man not as the result of imbibing culture but rather by reason of his high ideals and deep sentiments. He would sacrifice his own desires and urges to further the cause he espoused. He was so cultured as to disregard conventions so long as he could live and do what his conscience dictated. Pine's outstanding characteristic was: HATRED OF SHAM AND HYPOCRISY."

Judge Panken's opinion of Pine was shared by the entire labor movement. That was truly evidenced by the manner in which he was led to his eternal resting place.

It was the Judge Jacob Panken who also said that the Tailor Strike was the high-light of Max Pine's life. Referring to Pine, Judge Panken said:

"His contribution to the American Labor movement was no less than his contribution to the Tailors, maybe greater. The power of the Amalgamated was due to Pine's organizing, developing and strengthening the Tailors' Council and the organization and direction of the Tailor Strike. Not a speech, not an article was ever delivered or writen by Pine which did not urge constant and continued improvement of labor."

What pranks life plays! In answer to the author's letter asking for permission to open the Amalgamated archives to him in connection with his research—preparation of this book, the Director of Research of the Amalgamated, a letter dated November 24, 1947, wrote that "according to our records, Mr. Pine was never directly connected with the Amalgamated." Such is fame!

There are several reasons why the Tailor Strike that was proclaimed on December 30, 1912, was so important to the labor movement. In the first place, the number of strikers involved. One hundred thirty thousand struck, the largest number by far till then. In the second place, an entire industry was paralyzed for about two and one-half months. Third, it was believed impossible to organize the tailors. These immigrant tailors were formerly Yeshiva "bocherim" intelligentsia, teachers, bookkeepers, store-keepers, merchants, etc., all originally individualistic. They were not brought up on a cooperative philosophy of life. They were excellent objects of exploitation. Fourth, the United Garment Workers' Union, the then tailor union in America, looked down on the immigrant tailors. The American leaders of the United Garment Workers' Union disliked these immigrant tailors because they said that the American standard of living was undermined by them. The fact is that these immigrants brought about higher standards of living than those enjoyed by American labor: the eight-hour day was a dream—the immigrants made it a reality; the five-day week was unthought of by American unions—it was actually introduced by the needle industries largely composed of immigrants; the thirty-five hour week was first introduced in the needle industries by agreement made by Judge Panken between the employers and the Neckwear and Clothing workers and is now accepted by all.

It was these benefits that President Green of the A. F. of L. referred to as will be described in Chapter 4 following. Finally, after the successful cloakmakers' strike of 1910, an effort had to be made to unionize the men's clothing industry.

In May, 1911, Pine attended the convention of the few struggling tailor union locals. Eugene V. Debs, the Socialist Party leader, was the principal speaker. Then and there it was decided to organize the Tailor Council of the U. S. and Canada. Pine was elected the General Manager of the Tailor Council but refused to accept a paid position in the movement. The United Garment Workers' Union refused to recognize the Tailor Council and Brotherhood of Tailors. Finally, peace was made and the Council insisted that Pine, who was a very popular person among the masses of tailors, should organize the New York tailors. By the end of the summer of 1911, Pine was convinced that he was duty bound to accept the call to organize the tailors and he became the General Manager of the Tailor Council. Thomas A. Rickert, President, and Samuel Larger, Secretary, of the U. G. W. U. did not like Pine, for they claimed he was too radical and disapproved of the Tailor Council's functions and wanted it liquidated. But, despite said opposition, Pine's courage and perseverence, helped maintain the Tailor Council. Rickert and Larger then suggested Benjamin Schweitzer as Pine's co-organizer in order to have Schweitzer, the conservative, balance Pine, the radical. Schweitzer was acceptable to the Tailor Council, for he was a fine person. Judge Panken said "Schweitzer was appointed not for the purpose of adding fire to the revolt of the Tailors aroused by Pine, but rather to smother the flame—and it was a flame." Panken was counsel to the Tailor Council. Pine and Panken asked Rickert for financial aid, which was not forthcoming.

Pine, assisted by Schweitzer, worked among the tailors a full year to get them into unions. He carried on his activities with great enthusiasm. He wrote numerous fiery articles in "The Forward." Most of the spade work was done in the garment shops themselves. From his headquarters on 4th Street, in New York, he organized union locals throughout the metropolitan area.

By the end of November 1912, there were about 40,000 New York tailors organized. On December 14th, there appeared the first issue of the "Die Naye Tsait," the official organ of the Tailor Council. It called for a vote on a general strike. On December 21st, twenty-one mass meetings of tailors were held at which the strike was discussed and demands to the bosses formulated. Pine spoke at most of the important ones. A vote was taken and an overwhelming number voted for a strike declaration. Strike enthusiasm ran high. A large number of workers massed in Rutgers Square and Seward Park to hear the result of the vote. When Pine announced that the vast majority of the tailors voted "yes" the crowd began to shout, "Strike, Strike!" This enthusiasm had repercussions throughout the East Side. The scene was soul-stirring.

The "Strike Hagodol," as it was called, was declared by Pine on December 30, 1912. The day was cloudy and dull. Hundreds of shop committees of over 100,000 tailors distributed strike proclamations throughout the city. The response was warm. All Jewish, Italian, Polish, etc., tailors, men and women, as one person, left the shops and marched with enthusiasm and spirit to the appointed respective meeting halls during the 1st and 2nd days of the strike. In a week all shops were empty. The immigrant tailors had suddenly become first-page news in the English press. The strike was the greatest and most difficult in the history of the Jewish Labor Movement in America. The entire industry was paralyzed.

The demands were: 48 hour week; wage raises of $5.00 to $10.00 per week; recognition of the unions as the collective bargaining agent.

The bosses hired gangsters who severely injured many strikers and pickets. Injunctions were obtained against the pickets. The strike was a "Knockout" affair, no punches or holds barred. It is interesting to note that pickets faced danger at the price of a package of cigarettes a day.

At the "Forward" Editorial offices on East Broadway, there were two long tables where shop committee chairmen and all officers of the 25 local unions of the tailors sat together with the strike press committee. Bernard Weinstein, Secretary of the United Hebrew Trades issued the strike news—all about the picket lines, arrests, relief, shop settlements, etc.

Pine organized committees on picketing, on information, on fund collections, and a speakers' committee. Arrangements were made with grocers, bakers, barbers, for free groceries, bread and shaves for strikers and pickets.

After all the preparatory work for the strike had been completed, H. Lawner, the capable secretary of the N. Y. District Council of Tailors, affiliated with the United Garment Workers, appeared at the Forward Press Headquarters and offered help. The striking Jewish tailors did not like him because he was associated with the conservative U. G. W. U. and secondly, because he was a "cutter" of the upper strata of the workers in the clothing industry. The operators and finishers—rank and file—did not like cutters because cutters looked down on them. Rickert and Larger were also cutters. Lawner's offer of help was not accepted. Pine insisted that the United Hebrew Trades, to which he transferred the direction of the strike from the Tailor Council during the first week, should control the development of the great international tailor union of 130,000 tailors.

In refusing to accept Lawner's assistance, Pine said to Weinstein: "You, brother Secretary of the United Hebrew Trades, you saw how we conducted the entire ladies' waistmakers' strike in 1909; you saw our cloakmaker strike in 1910 when the U. H. T. did most of the work; you ran the furrier strike in 1912 and now, you, the U. H. T. must develop a great union in a great international of tailors."

The New York public was overwhelmingly sympathetic to the workers. The New York World particularly supported the cause of the strikers. It was the first great general strike in that important industry. The strikers were of all nationalities. The greatest number were Jews.

Next were the Italians with 25,000, then Lithuanians, Russians, Poles, Germans, Bohemians, Hungarians, Greeks, Turks, French, English and native-born Americans.

There were great demonstrations of these poor workers. During the second week of the strike, their poverty stood out in bold relief. Many didn't have enough to eat; many received dispossess notices because they could not pay rent. Free kitchens were opened where strikers could come for their daily meals. The Socialist Party members worked mostly in the free kitchens. The United Hebrew Trades, the Socialist Party, Workmen's Circles, the "Forward", all issued calls for help to all workers. The "Forward" gave thousands of dollars from its treasury to help the strikers. Adolph Held, manager of that newspaper, and later President of the Amalgamated Bank and now the Chairman of the Pension Fund of the I. L. G. W. U., did a great deal to help. Jacob Panken, William Karlin and Fiorello LaGuardia helped greatly. The I. L. G. W. U. then had 50,000 members and gave many thousands of dollars. All local unions organized functions, parties, affairs, balls, benefits, etc., where monies were collected. The U. G. W., when it saw the outstanding spirit of the strikers, changed its mind and called upon the A. F. of L. with which it was affiliated, to assist. All were then helpful.

The U. H. T. opened two grocery stores where flour, bread, sugar, beans, milk, etc., were distributed. It also opened a clothing distribution center at Clinton Hall for men, women and children. The Jewish Baker's Union provided thousands of loaves of bread daily for the free groceries and kitchens.

All monies collected by the U. H. T. were acknowledged in the "Forward" and turned over to the U. G. W. for distribution as strike benefits. The U. H. T. also held a great bazaar at the Forward Building for the benefit of the Strike Fund.

The struggle was long and bitter. Even DeLeon's Socialist Labor Party group helped. Although his group opposed the unions and wanted them destroyed, generally as we see elsewhere in this volume, DeLeon told Weinstein that the ''leaders of the Tailor Strike were not fakers but class-conscious workers of the struggling labor movement.''

Soon a number of small shops settled on the basis of a 50 hour week and small wage increases. At the end of the 8th week of the strike about 15,000 tailors were back at work in the settled shops. But the large manufacturers, organized in the three powerful associations, refused even to deal with the union. They refused to sit around the table with the union representatives of these ''green'' immigrants and particularly with the Socialists.

A committee of three public-spirited people consisting of Robert Fulton Cutting, a rich civic leader and a fine Christian; Marcus M. Marks, a Jewish-American communal leader, later President of the Borough of Manhattan; and Dr. Judah P. Magnes, former Rabbi at Temple Emanuel, New York, founder of Bnai Zion, the Fraternal Zionist Organization of America, and later President of the Hebrew University at Jerusalem, acted as mediators on behalf of the public.

The leaders of the large manufacturers' association could not refuse to discuss the issues of the strike with these outstanding and well-known personalities representing the public. The manufacturers refused to budge from their determination to have nothing to do with the unions. However, the committee was not to be denied a hearing. The men of the committee had spoken to Alfred Benjamin, the leader, and a group of large clothing manufacturers, heard their story in a friendly spirit and the manufacturers softened somewhat. The manufacturers agreed to yield on minor items such as a limitation to a 54 hour week and a wage increase of $1.00 per week. They refused absolutely to recognize the union as the collective bargaining agency.

The committee reported the results of the conversations to Rickert. The President called together the Executive Board of his union, the United Garment Workers, and they decided to accept the compromise believing that it was not a startling victory for the union, but it was a step forward.

Rickert recommended the acceptance of the settlement subject to the approval not of the strikers but of the "Forward", the leading Jewish daily under the editorship of Abraham Cahan. Pine and Schweitzer then appeared at Cahan's office Friday evening, February 28, 1913, to ask for his opinion.

Cahan argued that the compromise was a step forward, because the union as a union was for the first time actually in contact with the employers' associations—truly, not directly, but through mediators. He stated that the discussions could be considered as foundations for recognition of organized shops when the union would become stronger. He felt there was no alternative and that it was not a question of what is most satisfactory but rather of what is most needed. He reasoned that half a loaf was better than none.

Cahan described the conference in his memoirs thus:

"What do you say, comrade Cahan," Pine asked after he explained the matter.

"Accept the compromise," answered Cahan, "The Forward will be with you. It isn't a good settlement, but it can't be helped. At any rate, a strong union will be built."

"There will be many hot heads, they will set up a hue and cry. It will not go easy," said Pine. "People will realize that there was no other way out," Cahan answered.

Pine and Schweitzer reported to Rickert and the compromise was accepted and Rickert announced that the strike was settled on the terms above set forth.

The Forward of Saturday, March 1, 1913, ran a headline across five columns of page one. "The Great Tailor Strike is settled." The sub-title was: "The large Manufacturers' Associations yield at last on compromise."

That morning thousands gathered at Rutgers Square, Seward Park and in the lobby and the public halls of the "Forward". The air was filled with a spirit of protest, shock and disappointment. The protest reached the heights of rowdyism for the large windows of the front doors of the "Forward" were shattered.

The protest is described in the "Forward" of Sunday, March 2, 1913 under the headline: "Great Protest from the Tailors." The sub-title was: "Unhappy with the settlement." In the report of the situation, the "Forward" states: "Yesterday was an eventful day in the Tailor Strike. The news that the strike was settled brought great excitement not only from those who were happy with the compromise, but those who were not. The unhappy ones were the more vocal in proclaiming their protest. Large groups of strikers gathered at the meeting halls and around the offices of the strike—the Strike Committee then had its offices at the Bible House on 8th Street between 3rd and 4th Avenues, and debated the issues. Among the happy ones were principally those from the unsettled shops. Against the settlement were those of the settled shops.

"Around 12:00 o'clock, a large crowd gathered at the Forward Building, filling up the lobby and halls and denounced the "Forward". The windows were broken. This had a sad effect on the real union folk and these bitterly denounced these pogrom tactics. Such terroristic work is done by those who are ignorant and do not understand the value of a union. Union people do not believe in such arguments."

A conference was held at which were present leaders of the U. H. T., Forward Association, Arbeiter Ring (Workmen's Circle), and Socialist Party. It was determined to continue the strike and a committee was appointed to negotiate a new settlement. The committee consisted of: I. A.

Deutsch, Secretary of the I. L. G. W. U., Meyer London, Jacob Panken, Fiorello LaGuardia and D. Ashinsky of the Brotherhood of Tailors.

The strike was continued with renewed and greater effort and energy. There was a good deal of headbreaking during this period of the strike. The public reacted unfavorably to the continuance of the strike. Only the New York World supported the strikers. The public authorities condemned them. An appropriate illustration of the public disfavor is the following letter written on March 7, 1913, by Mayor William J. Gaynor to Ralph Waldo, Police Commissioner:

"Sir: I call your attention to the acts of lawlessness and violence which need to be put down by the police at all hazards at once. For many weeks there has been a strike in the garment making trade. That strike was settled a week ago by employers and the labor unions. As soon as such settlement was reached, Thomas A. Rickert, general President of the United Garment Workers of America, officially declared the strike at an end, and directed all employees to go back to work. This has been attested by Mr. Rickert and the representative of the employers' side, who have appeared before me. The settlement conceded practically all the demands of the employees. They did thereupon go back to work. But lawless persons have continued to hover around the factories and workshops ever since, and they are indulging in acts of lawlessness and violence. Two places have been shattered by bombs thrown by them and last evening Mr. Kohn of Washington Clothing Co. at 10 Astor Place, was knocked down and grievously battered and wounded by these lawless people after leaving his place of business for the day. These people are not engaged in any strike. They are lawless people in the City who come forward when there are strikes and disorders and commit all sorts of violence. Let them be dispersed. Let them not linger near these factories and places of business on the score that they are peaceful pickets. They are not pickets. The strike is at an end. They are lawless characters to whom no leniency whatever is due. See that they are not permitted to approach any of these factories and places of business. And let them be arrested if they commit any unlawful acts.

Very truly yours,

W. J. Gaynor, Mayor''

The following day both sides yielded and a compromise settlement was reached that was accepted by both sides. On March 8, 1913, the Great General Tailor Strike was settled on the following terms: All workers were to return to work; the work week was reduced to 53 hours till January 1, 1914 and 52 hours thereafter; cutters' work week was to be 50 hours till the end of the year and 48 hours thereafter; recognition of the union as the collective bargaining agency; salary increases of $4.00 to $6.00 per week.

The tailor strike proved false the argument of the United Garment Workers that the tailors could not be organized, particularly the immigrants. It was the outstanding example of what workers, through intelligent and efficient organization and spirited struggle could accomplish. It is important to note that as a result of the strike all locals of the United Garment Workers also became large and powerful. The workers who had joined the unions before and during the strike remained as members of the unions. Previously it had been that as soon as a strike was over the workers stopped paying dues and left the union. The Tailor Strike gave great impetus to the movement, for by the end of 1913, there was not a single trade employing Jews that was not organized into unions under the United Hebrew Trades which then had 107 local unions with over

200,000 members consisting of immigrant Jews, Italians, Poles, and native Americans.

The matter of the abortive settlement of the strike renewed the strained relations between the Tailor Council that organized the strike and the United Garment Workers, which still refused to accept the New York Coat Maker Locals into its union. The day of reckoning was at hand for the blind actions of the leadership of the U. G. W. brought about a revolution in the wheel of fate of the U. G. W. and it soon lost the leadership in the field of the clothing workers of America, soon these rejected immigrants caused the formation of the Amalgamated Clothing Workers Union, one of the most progressive and powerful unions in America.

All that developed at the following Convention of the United Garment Workers at Nashville, Tennessee, that opened on October 12, 1914. Nashville was not a clothing center and far from New York and other clothing centers. The convention city for 1914 had been adopted at the 17th convention at Indianapolis, in 1912. The successful New York tailors wanted the next convention to be held at Rochester, New York, a leading clothing center. Local 2 of the Brotherhood of Tailors submitted a written proposal to change the convention city to Rochester; four locals seconded the proposal. Under the U. G. W. constitution the matter had to be referred to all member locals for a referendum vote. Secretary Larger refused to hear the Committee of Local 2, for they feared a convention at a clothing center where these workers could send full representation.

The U. G. W. was composed of overall makers and tailors locals. The overall makers were mostly American born women who were told to beware of the tailors and their foreign elements, the Jews and Italians. The overall makers were more numerous than the tailors. The tailors were hoping for the opportunity to present the truth and to show that immigrant tailors had no horns and were people like the overall workers.

Pine was then stranded in Europe as the delegate of the United Hebrew Trades to the Second International Workers' Conference. The New York tailor delegation to the Nashville convention was led by Jacob Panken, its attorney. The U. G. W. leaders refused to seat the Brotherhood Tailors. Particular strife was had over Joseph Schlossberg of Local 39 of New York, who was then still associated with the Socialist Labor Party. He was called a revolutionary. But he was a delegate of the Joint Boards of the Brotherhood which had been organized by the 13 local tailor unions of New York soon after the great Tailor Strike. Schlossberg was willing to withdraw as a delegate if the others were recognized. But no, the tailors would not have it and the others refused them recognition.

The first day of the convention at the Capitol Hotel was peaceful. The Credentials Committee recommended the seating of all overall delegates and some tailor delegates, but refused to seat most of the tailor delegates from New York.

When Frank Rosenblum, a recognized delegate from Chicago asked if the report was final, the presiding officer answered "No" and the first session ended quietly.

The next morning only the recognized delegates were allowed on the convention floor and the tailor delegates were sent to the balcony reserved for visitors.

When Chairman Rickert announced the agenda, Frank Rosenblum moved a point of order that the convention was not ready to proceed with its business since a large number of delegates were not seated. Rickert overruled the point of order and Rosenblum appealed from the ruling of the chair. A vote was taken. A majority of the delegates in the convention hall voted to overrule the chair and sustain the point of order, but Rickert refused to count the vote of the tailors seated in the balcony and announced that his ruling was sustained and the point of order was declared overruled.

Delegate Pass of Chicago moved that since a minority of the convention took control of the convention, the convention should be moved to the Duncan Hotel and proceed with its business there. All Jewish tailor delegates thereupon left the Capitol Hotel and went to the Hotel Duncan. Hyman Schneid was elected temporary chairman and Samuel Sachs temporary secretary.

Discussions were held regarding the election of a permanent administration. Sidney Hillman of Local 39 of Chicago was proposed for the presidency. Since Hillman was not present, Panken 'phoned him and urged him to accept the presidency of the new tailor union. Hillman said "No!" But he was elected despite his refusal and Schlossberg was elected Secretary. Hillman then accepted the presidency. This group continued to call itself the United Garment Workers and decided to hold the 19th convention in 1916 at Rochester, New York.

The 34th Convention of the A. F. of L., of which the U. G. W. was an integral part, was held at Philadelphia, in November, 1914, right after the organization of the new U. G. W. under Hillman. Hillman decided to come to Philadelphia to the A. F. of L. Convention and present his grievances against the old U. G. W.

O'Connell of the machinists shouted, "Right or wrong, they must not be heard." The I. L. G. W. U., a member of the A. F. of L. proposed the appointment of a committee to investigate the entire dispute and to report. The proposal was voted down. The A. F. of L. declared war on the new organization. Pres. Samuel Gompers issued a circular to all locals demanding recognition of Rickert and Larger as the proper officers of the U. G. W. and directed the payment of per capita dues only to the old U. G. W.

Local 2 sent a letter to Gompers in which it stated that it recognized Hillman and Schlossberg as the officers of the U. G. W. to whom it would send all future correspondence and per capita dues.

All of the A. F. of L. unions started to expel tailors locals. Rickert and Larger obtained an injunction against the new and competing administration restraining it from using the name United Garment Workers of America.

Hillman called a special convention for December 25, 1914, at Webster Hall, New York City. There they changed the name to Amalgamated Clothing Workers of America.

The United Hebrew Trades, not being a union, did not belong to the A. F. of L., but most of the unions of the U. H. T. did belong. The A. F. of L. thereupon undertook to compel the U. H. T. to expel the Amalgamated delegates from its organization, warning that if they did not do so, the A F. L. would withdraw all its affiliated unions from the U. H. T. Gompers came to the meeting of the U. H. T. and personally issued the warning. Abraham Shiplacoff, then Secretary of the U. H. T. defended the Amalgamated. Gompers left that meeting in a huff. For the sake of peace, the Amalgamated voluntarily and formally withdrew from the U. H. T. Actually, however, it remained most friendly to the U. H. T.

Bernard Weinstein enumerated and summarized the winnings of the tailors thus:

1. Reduction of an average of seven hours per week for 130,000 workers, or about 900,000 work hours per week.

2. Employers' call to union for new workers.

3. Employers' call to union in event of shop labor dispute.

4. Abolition of the subcontractor or inside contractor. The old method was for the employer to give a quantity of work to one worker, who would hire helpers, mostly learners, whom he paid starvation wages and who worked these learners—newly arrived immigrants—as slaves.

5. Substantial increase in wages. In a shop visited by Weinstein, he asked each worker how much was his or her

increase in wages. Some answered $4.00 per week, some $6.00, some $8.00. There were some who earned $18.00 before the strike and $28.00 after the strike.

This was not a complete victory. It was, however, the beginning of a new day for the workers. It showed the road for the greater successes to come.

Pine was, therefore, in large measure responsible for the deliverance of the worker from slavery to freedom and from darkness to light. He set the ball rolling and as it rolled, it effected even greater improvements for labor; a step at a time but every step meant more for labor.

Chapter 4

PINE MEETS THE U. S. A.

To write about the life of Max Pine is to write not only the biography of one individual but also to write the history of the Jewish Labor movement in America. His life encompassed all that was of interest in the social, cultural, political and economic life of the Jewish laboring masses in America. His story describes the life and pictures the strife and anxiety in the struggle of the Jewish immigrant worker for a better life. It explains how unions were organized, how workers lived, how they carried on strikes, how their conditions improved. Pine's development was that of the Jewish immigrant worker from a "slave" to a dignified, self-respecting union worker, working 35 to 40 hours per week under excellent conditions, receiving the highest wages and enjoying the greatest freedom of any worker in the world.

The repressive and reghetoizing May 1881 Laws and the pogroms which ensued forced a great many Jews to leave Russia. Hundreds of Russian students calling themselves "Biluim" went to Palestine to colonize with the assistance of Baron Edmond Rothschild of France. Thousands went to Argentina to colonize the land purchased for them by Baron DeHirsch of England. Hundreds of thousands came to the U. S. A., the land of "milk and honey" where "gold is found in the streets." Between 1881 and 1886 some 77,000 Jews came here. Between 1887 and 1892, 243,687 Jews landed here.

Pine was one of those who left Russia and arrived at the New York Castle Garden in the year 1890.

Castle Garden was then in its last year as the port of entry before becoming the New York City Aquarium. It was swamped with immigrants. The Commissioners of Immigration were warm-hearted men who removed all stumbling blocks to the entrance of these refugees. There was then no quota system and no Walter-McCarran Act. The immigrants were permitted to remain in Castle Garden for days, sleeping on the floor or on boards as best as they might, with such covering as was on hand or as kindly people in the city provided. Although it was merely a gateway through which people could enter the U. S. A., Castle Garden actually was turned into a lodging place, for many had to be kept there to be cured of trachoma and other diseases and until some kind people would come to receive them.

Most Jewish life was then centered on the East Side, bounded on the south by Henry Street, on the east by Pitt Street, on the north by Houston Street, on the west by the Bowery. It was later expanded so that it was bounded on the south and on the east by the East River and on the north by East 14th Street. More than 300,000 Jewish souls lived in the original East Side and some 600,000 lived in the enlarged East Side. Grand Street was the Fifth Avenue of downtown Jewry. On the Sabbath and Jewish Holidays the street was crowded with people dressed in their ''sunday best.''

The East Side atmosphere to which these immigrants were brought was foul. There were tenements which had bedrooms without light or air; cesspool water closets were in the yards facing the windows of the rear tenements; children played in filthy yards; youngsters of tender age mixed with gangsters of evil habits; on every block there were three or four cigar stores and ''cider stubes'', in the rear of which harlots plied their trade; work in sweat shops, which will be described later, was the order of the day.

Pine found on his arrival the following Political, Labor, Social and Cultural conditions:

POLITICAL

Benjamin Harrison was President of the United States. He had defeated President Grover Cleveland, although President Cleveland received over 100,000 more popular votes than he. Although this election started a movement to amend the constitution of the U. S. by abolishing the Electoral College and have Presidents elected by popular vote, it is now 1959 and that amendment is still a long way off.

The census of 1890 reported a population of 62,947,714 people as compared to 150,697,361 in 1950. The U. S. census director estimated a population of more than 170,000,000 people in 1957.

North and South Dakotas and Montana were admitted to the Union in 1889; Idaho and Wyoming in 1890; thus establishing for the first time an unbroken tier of northern states from the Atlantic to the Pacific.

The McKinley Tariff increased duties on all goods and started the heated debate on whether or not a high tariff is good for the general economy of our country and thus is good or bad for labor.

The Sherman Anti-Trust Act was passed. It declared that "every contract, combination in the form of a trust or otherwise, or conspiracy or restraint of trade among the several states or with foreign nations" was illegal. Our courts are still busy interpreting the terms "combination", "conspiracy", "restraint" and "trade", and now in 1959 the Attorney General of the United States is still trying to convict the Atlantic & Pacific Tea Company, the largest grocery chain in the world, for a violation of the law.

The City of New York (then only Manhattan and Bronx Boroughs) had gone through an interesting and exciting mayoralty campaign. New York City was not formed by unification until January 1, 1898.

One Ludwig Yablinowsky of the cigar makers' Union Local #90—contrary to the established policy of the American Federation of Labor which was organized in 1881 and which had as its President, Samuel Gompers, another cigar maker, proposed that the Central Labor Union of New York should enter the political field. Although the Socialists were the leaders of that movement, they had no candidate of their own. Therefore, they had to find their candidate outside their ranks, from among the liberals. Henry George, originally a typesetter, who, by personal pluck and study became a philosopher, a thinker, an economist, a reformer, a brilliant pamphleteer and agitator, the founder of the Single Tax Theory and whose book "Progress and Poverty", wherein he attacked the then modern society, created a sensation, was the chosen candidate of the third party, known as the United Labor Party in 1886. The campaign was heated. Labor, liberals and socialists joined for the first time as a labor party. His Republican and Democratic opponents were Theodore Roosevelt and Abram S. Hewitt respectively. Hewitt was elected with 90,552 votes, but Henry George ran ahead of Teddy Roosevelt with 68,110 to 60,435.

After the election there developed a bitter struggle for control of the United Labor Party between the Single Taxers and the Socialists. At the annual convention of the United Labor Party at Syracuse the following year, Henry George won and the Socialists were practically expelled from the party.

Father McGlynn took an active part in the George mayoralty campaign. The Catholic leadership warned McGlynn to leave the third party movement. Upon his refusal he was excommunicated and "unrobed". German and Jewish Socialists leaders organized a demonstration of solidarity with McGlynn.

Another who took an active part in the George campaign was Daniel DeLeon who later became the leader and then the attacker of the Socialist Party. He was a lecturer on International Law at Columbia University. He remained with the party after the Socialists were expelled. When George's Labor Party was liquidated, DeLeon joined the Socialist Labor Party. More about him later.

LABOR

In the beginning of the Jewish Labor movement in America, a bitter struggle for the control of labor was going on between the Socialists and Anarchists, similar to the present bitter struggle for control of labor between the Socialists and the Communists. To a Socialist the greatest enemy of the working class is not the capitalist or employer but the Communist. To a Communist, the greatest enemy of the working class is not the capitalist or employer, but the Socialist. The Communist calls the Socialist a Fascist, reactionary and the betrayer of the working class in its struggle for a new and better life and a free world.

In these early days, the Labor headquarters were at Red Star Hall, 165 East Broadway, where public meetings, lectures and debates were held every Sunday afternoon on the subjects of Socialism, Anarchism and the labor movement in general. Louis Miller and M. Zametkin led the Social Democrats and Roman Lewis, M. Girsdansky, S. Yanovsky and Dr. H. Zolotaroff led the Anarchists. The Anarchists insisted upon arming the workers. The Social Democrats opposed. The battle was so heated that there were almost inter-labor fights in many shops.

The language used at these meetings, lectures and debates was Russian. Abraham Cahan was on the side of the Social Democrats. He, too, spoke in Russian interspersed with English and Yiddish idioms.

Finally, there was a split in the organization which sponsored these meetings and which was then known as the "Russian Progressive Soyuz", and the Social Democrats joined the Socialist Labor Party by organizing Branch #8.

This was the beginning of Jewish Socialist propaganda in America.

The Anarchists formed a society called "Pioneers for Freedom" with headquarters at 56 Orchard Street. Branch 8 of the S. L. P. met at 10 Hester Street. Meetings of both groups were held at the same time on Friday evenings. For a time the Anarchists, who were more energetic and practical, were more successful and drew the larger audiences. But in time even some of the Anarchists saw the light and became Social Democrats, for whom Abraham Cahan was then the principal and favorite speaker.

In 1888 the United Hebrew Trades was organized. It played an important role in the development of the Jewish Labor movement in America and about which we shall write at length later. The delegates who formed the U. H. T. were from Branch 8 of the S. L. P., choristers' union, actors' union and typesetters' union. They undertook to form new unions. The organization of the new unions helped the U. H. T. to outstrip the Anarchists and the United German Trades, from which it took its name.

The struggle was renewed in the Socialist Labor Party, which was originally a purely German party. The official national publication was the "Socialist", published in German at the Labor Lyceum Building at 25 East 4th Street. The meetings were conducted in German and German Socialist songs were sung. The Socialists attacked the non-Socialist unions. The daily "Volkzeitung", not a S. L. P. organ, with which were associated Johnas and Shevitch, who were the leaders of the S. L. P. opposed the attack. They believed the party needed the unions and should not alienate them or attack them but on the contrary, it should try to win them over. They argued that that was the best method to teach Socialism to labor. The "Workman's Advocate", whose editor, Busche, attended the Second International Socialist Congress in Paris in the summer of 1889, was purchased by the S. L. P. and under the editorship of Lucien Sanial, sided with the "Socialist" and opposed the "Volkzeitung."

A great Socialist Labor Party meeting was held on a Sunday afternoon at Clarendon Hall in 13th Street, between 3rd and 4th Avenues, to discuss the problems of the unions. Practically all the speeches were in German. Shevitch and Hugo Focht delivered brilliant addresses attacking the party leadership. Abraham Cahan sided with them but spoke in English. A vote was taken and Shevitch and Focht won overwhelmingly.

A break followed and two Socialist Labor Parties co-existed, each claiming that it was "the" Socialist Labor Party. A German named Rosenberg, the leader of the "Socialist" anti-union group moved his headquarters and the paper to Cincinnati. The "Volkzeitung" refused to move to Cincinnati and remained in New York. Busche and the "Workmen's Advocate", although in the minority and agreeing with Rosenberg, also remained in New York. But soon thereafter, at a meeting of the Publishing Association, Busche was deposed as editor and Sanial elected to replace him.

American Labor was organized in the Knights of Labor, founded in 1869 and American Federation of Labor founded in 1881. But both refused to help the immigrant; in fact they would not for many years admit a union composed of immigrants. These American Labor leaders looked down on the immigrants as cheap labor from Eastern Europe come to reduce the American standard of living. How wrong these leaders were. It took many years of unpleasant strife to convince them that these newcomers did belong with them. When they did admit them to their union and did work with them, they finally admitted their error to their regret.

The year 1890 is recorded as the year of the first great cloak-maker strike. A committee consisting of Joseph Barondess, chairman, Bernard Weinstein and M. Schack were organizing the cloakmakers, with headquarters at 92 Hester Street. Many were joining the unions. Some manufacturers retaliated and on May 19, 1890, locked out all their workers. The remaining cloak makers then called a strike in sympathy with those locked out. The cutters complained to the District Attorney and presented evidence to the Grand Jury that the manufacturers violated Sections 168 and 171 of the Penal Code by conspiring to prevent union members from pursuing their trade "by the utterance of threats and other intimidations and also by locking out all of their employees until their union would end the strike in the Meyer Jonasson & Company's factories and each employee withdrew from the Union." The June Grand Jury refused to indict, so did the July jury. The New York World assailed the Grand Juries as "setting up the precedent that what was conspiracy on the part of the workingman was not a crime when resorted to by the capitalists." It published a scathing editorial (7/12/90) entitled, "The Rights of Man," in which it condemned the thought that there was one law for the rich and another for the poor.

The struggle between employers and employees was a life and death struggle. Those locked out and those striking suffered greatly. Though public opinion was with the strikers, only small sums were raised. At one of the distribution points for the strikers there "was no more than $350.00 to be divided among over 4,000 persons and a large majority were sent away empty handed." (New York Tribune 7/12/90.)

The workers' "showed plainly the pinch of hunger on their faces" in spite of their large beards. (7/9/90.)

On July 15, 1890, an agreement was entered into between the cloakmaker manufacturers and Thomas Garside, a former S. L. P. member, an anarchist and then President of the Cloakmakers' Union which provided for recognition of the unions, settlement of disputes by arbitration, strikers to be reemployed and cutters to be paid for lost time. Chief demands that were not acceptable to the employers were: 1. discharge of scabs and 2. settled prices for piece work. The settlement agreement, having been written in the English language, was brought to Abraham Cahan for translation. When the workers heard the terms of acceptance and rejections, they met at New Everett Hall, 31 East 4th Street, and held a protracted meeting. The cutters, who were happy with getting back pay, decided to go back to work. A vote was taken and 1536 voted against acceptance of the agreement and 20 voted to accept it. Great enthusiasm followed. The decision was made to continue the strike. Rings, watches, earrings, bracelets and other pieces of jewelry were given to the chairman to carry on the strike. Ten days later the strike was settled with complete victory for the workers.

The police were most unfriendly. Chief Police Inspector Byrnes wrote, "I will reach out my hand and shake them as I would a lot of rats."

The courts, too, were unsympathetic. In Essex Market Court, Judge Duffy in admonishing arrested strikers, declared that "no man has a right to fix wages for others" and that if the cloak strike had happened in Russia, the strikers would have been sent to Siberia." "We have no Siberia in America" he added, "But we have laws and you can be sent to prison." (N. Y. World 7/24/90.)

The manufacturers made every attempt to put obstacles in the path of the immigrants and to intimidate them. Many arrests were made during the strike and many after victory in order to discourage the workers and their leaders. But they were not to be discouraged.

SOCIAL AND CULTURAL

The leading Jewish publication was the "American Hebrew" which was first published on November 21, 1879. On April 4, 1890, the "American Hebrew" published a "Symposium on Prejudice Against the Jews, its Nature, its Causes and its Remedy." All contributors to the "Symposium" were leading non-Jews and it attracted worldwide attention. The "American Hebrew" was in the forefront to protect the Jewish name and honor. The struggle between the Socialists and Anarchists referred to above had its analogy in the struggle in the upper strata of the Jewish community, between those who were interested only in themselves and those interested in the welfare of the Jewish community.

In a letter dated July 16, 1890, addressed to Philip Cowen, publisher of the magazine, Jacob H. Schiff wrote:

"I have noticed with much regret that in the festivities arranged during last week in honor of the Russian warships at this port, Messrs. Theodore Myers, Ferdinand Levy and A. DeFreece made themselves most prominent. Have we a right to ask of our neighbors in behalf of our Russian co-religionists and the condemnation of the oppressors if we hasten to do honor to those who come here officially representing the Czar's government? A word of censure in the American Hebrew would not be out of place and at the same time present the impression from going abroad that New York Jews are wanting in self-respect."

In the field of Jewish education there was the infant "The Jewish Theological Seminary" that was founded in 1886. This was a school of higher Jewish education where young men studied for the rabbinate.

In 1890, Dr. Joseph I. Bluestone and Rabbis Philip Klein, Aaron Wise, father of the recently departed Rabbi Stephen S. Wise, H. Pereira Mendes and M. S. Margolis, formed an organization known as Shovai Zion, which soon became the leading society working for the redemption of Palestine as the Jewish Homeland. It is interesting to note that Dr. Joseph I. Bluestone and Dr. Judah P. Magnes, helped found Bnai Zion, then known as Order Sons of Zion, the Fraternal Zionist Organization of America, which in 1944 elected Harry A. Pine, Max Pine's son, to the presidency.

The first American settlement house was founded by Stanton Coit, in 1886, as Neighborhood Guild, with headquarters at 146 Forsyth Street. There the boys and girls of the neighborhood learned Americanism to improve themselves. It soon became the headquarters of all neighborhood needs, activities and civic enterprises. Charles B. Stover, later Park Commissioner under Mayor Gaynor, was the leading spirit of the movement which adopted the name of University Settlement.

Dr. Nicholas Murray Butler described the University Settlement as the "veritable lighthouse on the East Side."

Mrs. Eleanor Roosevelt traced her interest in people's welfare to her experience during two years' residence at the University Settlement. At the 60th Annual Banquet of the University Settlement at the Waldorf-Astoria, Mrs. Roosevelt told how a tall young man used to come to the settlement to take her out for an evening and how the young girls used to say to her, "isn't that your feller?" and how she replied, "No, he is my cousin,"—and that cousin was none other than the person who later became her husband, Franklin Delano Roosevelt.

Such was the America, such was the East Side into which Max Pine found himself upon his arrival in 1890.

Chapter 5

PINE MEETS THE SWEAT SHOP

The Jewish immigrants who flocked to the land where "gold and silver were found in the streets," landed with no assurance of a job. The United States Employment Bureau had not yet been set up. Neither were State Employment Bureaus. There were yet no national or local organizations for distribution and placement of labor. Being ignorant of our language and of our economic opportunities, they had to shift for themselves to find places in our American life as best they could and had to resort to all sorts of devices.

They used to meet on street corners and in the public parks and these became the improvised labor markets known as the "Chazar Marks."

Upon Pine's arrival, he was chosen at the "Pig Market" for a job in a coal yard where he worked several months. He was young and strong and had no difficulty in carrying the pails and sacks of coal to the fourth and fifth floors of the tenements.

He attended his first workers' meeting, that of the Architectural Iron Workers, on Delancey Street, near the Bowery. Those present were mostly Germans, with a sprinkling of Jews. There he met Bernard Weinstein who was at that time Secretary of the United Hebrew Trades, who spoke in Yiddish and with whom he became an intimate friend for the remainder of his life.

Then a friend induced him to come with him to a kneepants' factory on the fourth floor of a Hester Street building and learn to become an operator. Pine described the place in which he was introduced to the sweatshop thus:

"The day was cloudy and dull; in the shop we worked with hanging lamps; I noticed the three little rooms that made up the 'factory' and the living quarters of the 'boss.' At the entrance was the kitchen with a large cast-iron stove on which were a number of heavy red hot press irons. In the next room, the largest—the living room—there were 9—10 sewing machines tightly squeezed together and the operators seemed glued to their seats. The contractor came to me, looked me over and a smile appeared on his face.

'A strong youngster,' he said, 'red cheeks, a good appetite, you'll be all right in America.'

"Standing there we made the bargain. I was to give him $25.00 and would work three weeks without pay during my apprenticeship.

"As I put my hand in my pocket to take out the $25.00, my hand seemed paralyzed. My gaze fell upon a little thin emaciated looking operator who squirmed at the machine as if he were a living creature in deathly pain. In a moment I wanted to run away from this hell-hole. I didn't think more than a moment and the matter became clear to me. What will I do? I am alone, strange, have no one; in a short time I will eat up my savings, my shoes and clothing will tear. What will I do then? I decided to remain, paid the money and stayed.

"Each morning before dawn I arrived at the shop and left late at night, broken up with heavy heart and aching bones.

"The three weeks were over and I then earned $1.00 a day for making 60 knee-pants. That was the regular price. The day was long, many times it seemed as though it lasted two days."

This was a sweat shop common to the needle industries. A New York State Factory Inspector described one of the shops he visited:

"Three rooms and a kitchen, the living room was a sewing shop and in the other two rooms lived the contractor and his wife, mother-in-law and seven children. In the kitchen was a stove used for the pressers' press irons; rack for finished cloaks, bundles of cut-up work, work tables; in the corner of the kitchen the woman was kneading dough for 'chaleh' (white bread twist), the floor was filthy."

Another factory inspector's description of a sweat shop is:

"In basement, dark low dirty cellar, workroom 14' x 14' 7½" high, 4 sewing machines, hot coal stove for press irons; 4 men and 3 women workers; next room, a kitchen used as living room for contractor and family. He also had two boarders who slept in the shop."

The conditions of labor in these shops were revolting. The hours of labor were long and the wages were low. The New York Board of Labor Statistics reported shop conditions in a woman's garment shop:

"Many obnoxious shop rules were in force. For instance, before new spools of silk were given out, the old empty spools had to be returned; if they were lost, a fine of 50 cents had to be paid for each, the real value being nothing; for the loss of a number ticket the fine was 25¢; if an employee lost a 'trimming' ticket before he even had received the trimmings, he had to pay the full value of the trimmings, which were valued from $1.00 to $10.00; it was as though he had lost the trimmings and not the ticket; the ticket cost an extra fine of 25¢; for the loss of a special ticket the fine was 50¢ to 75¢; in some shops it was forbidden to bring cooked meals from home; this was a great hardship for the poor worker; in some shops they were not allowed to drink beer; workers were discharged for coming in five minutes late, or stopping five minutes too soon; weekly workers were fined three hours' pay for coming in one-half hour late.''

These sweat shops were operated by small irresponsible contractors in these dark, filthy lofts of tenements and in these airless, lightless cellars, with no toilet facilities and no rest rooms or rest places. The shops were fire hazards. Children of tender age would work in the factories to sew on buttons or pull out bastings. In many shops the contractor distributed work to be done at home after their regular long hours. The worker would load the batch of the cut goods into a sack, detach the 'head' of his sewing machine from the stand and put it also into the sack. Then the worker swung the sack onto his back for the walk home. These sacks were called ''Black Bags of Infamy.'' On arrival home he fixed the machine ''head'' on a stand and began to work again. His wife and children helped him. In the morning, before dawn, he placed the ''head'' and the finished work in the same black sack and lugged it back to the shop. The machines belonged to the workers who either bought them or hired them at $1.50 per week. The workers carried them on their backs from shop to shop. In addition to supplying their own machines, the workers had to pay for the machine oil, the leather belt, needles and cotton and silk thread. For all this they were paid pitifully small starvation wages. Ten dollars a week was a top salary. The majority received between $5.00 and $10.00 for an 83 hour week. Women earned $3.50 per week.

In order to earn more so that they could pay their rent—many workers were being dispossessed because they didn't earn enough for rent and other bare necessities—many a worker had the other members of his family work, even his minor children. In many instances parents had to falsify children's ages so that they could get working papers for them. Most homes had to take in boarders to supplement the family income.

By reason of the bitter economic struggle, prostitution was rife on the East Side. At first white slavery was practiced secretly, later it was protected, assisted and encouraged by the evil politicians. Then the prostitutes came out into the open and on the street. At first the women would attract their prey by the clanging of their keys; later, they put red objects on the doors of their houses. Soon the red lights were so numerous in the streets where immigrants lived that the district was called the "red light district."

Baking bread and candy making were done in basements and cellars in tenements. Gregory Weinstein, an old East Side civic worker, in his book, "The Ardent Eighties and After" described a bakery he visited:

"In one of the cellar bakeries we found a baker asleep on the table, with his head sunk into a mass of bread dough. A black cat shared his pillow." The poor overworked bakers had no other clothes than those rags they wore when they worked.

To sum up: These sweat shops had the following characteristics: The workers received low wages; worked long hours under unsanitary condition; the contractors speeded up the workers; the entire worker family did not earn enough to make a living; workers were degraded to the level of beasts or machines; unemployed workers gathered in these "Pig Markets" where the bosses could have their pick of the lowest bidder; home work was the order of the day for the workers. The husband, wife and children would work at all hours.

These conditions bred disease and caused degeneration of the worker and his family. These workers were hollow-eyed, thin and stooped. Their steady music was the hacking cough of tuberculosis for the workers' lungs were infiltrated with lint. Their children had rickets and showed it.

The poem, "The Aged Tailor", by Morris Rosenfeld,
the great Yiddish Socialist poet, well describes these
"slaves":

THE AGED TAILOR

English translation by SHOLOM J. KAHN

These many years he has been sitting,
pale face sweating as he sews,—
like the cotton he is threading
is the white his beard now shows.
In town there's hardly a master
to whom his work has not been lent,
yet there's no bread for wife and children,
in his wallet, not a cent.
He comes to the shop in early morning
to sell his handiwork for pay;—
he keeps on always, always earning,
not a penny's thrown away.
Already at work when dawn is graying,
still he labors late at night,
but always, always, sadly thinking
where to borrow for his plight.
In him the boss finds satisfaction:
few the arguments he's made;
he's not the one to raise a tumult
nor belittle his own trade.
He comes and goes away in silence;—
yet his cough speaks without rest!
The tears are hidden by his glasses,
and the pain, within his breast.
In all the workers, when their glances
catch the sick one, sorrow grows;
they all watch his weary shoulders
bending over while he sews.
They see already death's dark verdict,
punishment for his honesty . . . .
They see, reflected as in a mirror,
in his age, their destiny.

These were the conditions under which Pine commenced his career in the needle industry. He at once saw the need of improving his own conditions and those of his fellow workers.

One evening, after work, Pine and his friend went to a rear house in Broome Street, the office of the then infant knee-pants makers' union and joined up. After he had registered with the union, he was met by his boss who had spied on him.

That night Pine could not sleep, for it was very risky then to join a union. He was worried about the matter. Where could he get work—he was not yet a proficient worker? Besides, he would have to carry around his "Katerinka" (play box) machine on his shoulder until he could get another job.

On his arrival at the "factory" the following morning, he noticed that he had no cut-up bundles at his table. That was a bad omen. The boss came over, gave him a nasty look and wanted to strike Pine, but was held back by some other workers. Pine was thereupon discharged. Immediately all the workers started to remove the heads of their machines and break up the stands, packed hurriedly and put the machines in the hallway. As they stood in the hallway, the presser, who had been sent by the boss as his "ambassador of goodwill" appeared and said, "The boss is sorry! He wants to take back the green operator (Pine) and wants you all to return to work, and in order to show his goodwill and make peace, he will set up a barrel of beer."

The workers answered that they didn't want his beer and refused to go back to work. They said they were on strike and demanded that the boss come to them and they'll tell him what they wanted. An operator used a machine table for a desk and wrote out the demands: "they were striking; they wanted a nickel more per dozen pants; the boss was to recognize the union; they were not to carry the bundles of work from the truck to the 4th floor factory; they should receive their pay every two weeks instead of at the will of the boss; the boss was to bring the machines and install them at the stands; the wife of the boss was no longer to curse the workers.''

The boss appeared and yielded, and the workers won the strike and all their demands. Since that victory was the result of the Pine episode, Pine became the shop hero. He was asked to say something. As Pine described it: ''My heart beat heavily and I don't remember what I said because I was so frightened.''

This had been his maiden speech in America. He soon developed into one of the most gifted speakers in the entire labor movement. When he finished his speech, he was unanimously elected shop delegate. The following Friday the entire shop went to the union to join. This was the beginning of his activity as a leader in the Knee-Pants Makers' Union.

These early days of the Jewish labor movement in America were soul-stirring and full of bitter strife. One of the most heart-breaking and disappointing experiences was described by Pine in an article, entitled, ''When a Brother Becomes a Boss.'' In that knee-pants' shop the boss was making Pine's friend, Gedalia, the presser, his partner and appointed Pine as one of two appraisers to appraise the shop in order to determine how much Gedalia was to pay the boss for one-half of it. At that time Gedalia was already reading the ''Tageblatt'' (Jewish Daily) which attacked the workers. It was called a capitalist paper.

Now that Gedalia, the presser, became a boss, things became worse. There was to be no more singing in the shop; peddlers could no longer bring lunch and cigarettes into the shop; neither could newsboys sell their papers; the boss would throw these men out. Gedalia continued to press and made his co-pressers miserable. Although he shared the work with them he took the smaller sizes and gave the others the large ones. Since wages were paid per piece made, Gedalia got the best of the bargain.

At one of the union meetings, Pine met Abraham Cahan, who was the pioneer and guiding spirit of Jewish journalism and Socialism. He had known him in his home town of Weilitch, where Cahan was a teacher in the government school for Jewish children. He was astonished to see the intellectual Cahan mix with the plain people, ordinary workers, and Pine, then and there, decided to devote his life to the welfare of the working class. He took an oath that he would dedicate himself to work on behalf of the ''human slaves'' and be true to them to his last breath.

Pine, like the other pioneer labor leaders, did not become tired or discouraged when unions were formed after great effort and energy and fell apart like a house of cards. These men, after giving up their energy to work for a living for themselves and their families, worked with almost supernatural zeal to organize and help others.

These were the conditions which Pine had to contend with on his road to improve the lot of the worker.

Chapter 6

THE LABOR LEADER

Pine soon became a courageous brave union leader who shouted at his fellow knee-pants' workers, "Let us give up carrying our 'Katerinkes' (machines) on our shoulders from shop to shop. The bosses must give us machines on which to work." Upon his elevation to leadership in the knee-pants makers' union, now a vital part of the Amalgamated Clothing Workers Union, he organized and directed the strikes of 1891 and 1892. Pine was called the "Moses" of the union. The strikes were successfully concluded from Pine's headquarters at Valhalla Hall, 60 Orchard Street, the largest hall on the East Side.

An interesting debate took place when he was nominated for union leadership. He was not a very good operator, being considered a "botcher" who could not make a "pistol pocket." The "experts", the old-timers, therefore, objected to his election. So, too, did the "genossen", intellectual socialists. But the rank and file liked him and elected him.

Some demands of the union were: machines, press cloths, needles and thread to be supplied by the bosses; also higher wages. The machine demand was made after a great deal of discussion and opposition. The workers who owned their own machines opposed the demand and opposed the strike. However, at a meeting of the strike committee Pine bowled them over with a story. He told them that in a certain city the City Council was debating a bill to lower the fare from ten cents to five cents. The workers protested that they were not satisfied because they said, 'when it cost ten cents to ride and we walked, then we saved ten cents; but now, if we will walk, we'll only save a nickel, so that we would lose a nickel by this resolution.' This witticism was the best argument and carried the day.

As an example and as an inspiration to the strikers, Pine joined the picket lines and was with the strikers day and night. Demands were also made for written agreements also that the manufacturers should guarantee for the contractors the wages and working conditions of the workers. The latter was an important innovation for in many instances the workers slaved in these sweatshops for the contractors and after a few weeks' work, the contractor would disappear and the workers would go unpaid.

The 1891 strike was a bitter one for there were no real unions to help this single union. The strike motto was "work and starve or fight and starve." The workers chose the latter. There were many street fights. Strikers walked around with bandaged heads and battered noses. Picketing was dangerous business, but the union was never short of pickets.

A great struggle centered about a shop on the Bowery and Bayard Street. The owner's wife put stones in boiling water and she and her scabs used to attack the pickets with the red hot stones. Many pickets were sent to the hospitals.

The strikers met day and night and worked in sections— while some picketed the others slept and vice versa. At night the union headquarters looked like a military barrack lit by two gas lights. Several hundred strikers slept on the floor, many with wounds.

From a monetary point of view, to win the strike meant merely a few additional pennies, but it was the idealism of these first Socialists and their leader Pine, which enthused the workers and gave them courage to hunger and struggle and go all out for the strike.

Pine talked, preached, taught and pleaded with the Kneepants' makers. He instilled in them the spirit of struggle against the enemies of the working class and he stated that every strike, every combat with capitalism, was of the utmost importance in the speeding of that great day when mankind will be freed from economic slavery. He explained that this strike was a struggle not only for more bread but also for the preparation of an army of workers in the class struggle for that last fight that will bring light, joy and freedom to the entire world.

The union won that strike. First, a number of the leading manufacturers signed up and the rest followed. The knee-pants' workers' union then became the model and most progressive union in the needle industry. All other unions soon demanded that Pine help them too. He was invited to and did speak at union meetings of other trades. He helped the others in all their strikes.

At a large meeting of pants' makers at the Irving Hall on Broome Street, Pine spoke about the time to come when the workers will win an eight hour day. He noticed a cold response. He thought to himself that these slave workers thought he was a dreamer. After the meeting a man approached Pine to congratulate him and said, ''These animals did not understand you. But I did. They can't understand that such a thing as an eight-hour day is possible. They figure that since they can't make a living on 16 hours a day, how will they do it on 8? The damned fools don't understand that if there will be an 8 hour day, then one will be able to work for two bosses, 8 hours each and get double pay.''

To be a labor leader was difficult business. Leaders had plenty of difficulty in keeping the unions they organized from disintegrating. In many instances, as soon as a union would get some money an unfaithful secretary would disappear with it and that would be the end of the union until another was formed after much sweat and hard work.

An interesting episode was told by Pine about a Baker Union meeting to which he and two others came to represent the United Hebrew Trades. The problem that was most urgent was the report of the Secretary of the Union. He had no money and no receipts. He had disbursed the money and burned the receipts. He was asked why he burned the receipts and answered, "I didn't need them any longer after I paid out the money."

When one of the delegates suggested that a crime had been committed and that the law would have to take its course, a union "bully", a friend of the Secretary yelled, "Mister, who are you?" The delegate answered, "I was sent by the U. H. T."

"Why didn't the United Hebrew Trades itself come here? I would have taken his eye out."

There gas a great laughter among the members. Several instances of tumult developed. "I'll kill him, this United Hebrew Trades", said the bully."

"Throw him out," rang through the hall.

Each one accused the other of being a thief. There developed a free for all fight which overflowed into the street. The chairman was beaten up and one of the U. H. T. delegates had both eyes blackened.

Today unions are taken for granted. They are legally and morally recognized. In those early days there was no recognition. Employers were bitter enemies of the unions and of those intending to organize labor. They fought every attempt to better working conditions. Employers believed that American freedom meant freedom to exploit under the Sweat Shop system.

To become a union man was risky enough for the worker because he knew that when his employer would learn about it he would lose his job.

But to become a labor leader was to risk one's very life. Then it was the general rule. Nowadays, in the case of Walter Reuther, it is the exception. Only the compulsion of the highest form of idealism enabled Pine to carry on to help organize and lead in the labor movement. The unions were physically weak, they had few members and no money. Many leaders died of weariness and shock. Pine was young and strong. Work piled on work and each of the groups he helped organize left its mark which was used as a starting point by its successor.

It was very difficult to strike in New York. In addition to the problems with the bosses themselves as described above, there were problems with the police and the courts. Strikes were forbidden by injunctions, so too, were picketing, the holding of meetings, the distribution of leaflets and strike calls. Unions were also ordered disbanded by injunction. Police permitted gangsters to beat up strikers and pickets. Strikers risked their lives on appearance, more so on picketing. It was normal for employers to hire "bums" and gangsters to fight the strikers.

The unions not only had to fight back fire with fire but also had to propagandize their cause and explain the rights of labor to strike and picket. They also had to fight the conservative Yiddish press. An example of the hatred toward the unions and the strikers is the following excerpt of a circular distributed by a conservative Yiddish daily: "Just look how the workers became wild. It is not enough that they have enough bread and butter to eat, they also want a piece of ham so that they could eat "Traife" sandwiches. The paper threatened the workers that they would be sent back to Europe.

To contrast the said vicious attitude of the said daily, it is interesting to note what that great liberal Rabbi Stephen S. Wise said of these workers who crowded his Friday evening services which he conducted for the Free Synagogue at Clinton Hall, on Clinton near Grand Street.

"Who were these people. No man could have preached to a more friendly intelligent group, deeply concerned about Jewish and general problems, religious, racial, political."

Pine was in great demand as an organizer and speaker. Some local unions which Pine helped either as an organizer or in their strikes founded the I. L. G. W. U. in 1900.

In 1902 he helped form the union of Jewish writers in New York City and was elected its first secretary.

He went from union to union. He helped organize strikers and helped in those strikes. He was a leader in practically all of the strikes of the New York City Jewish workers. In 1906 he was one of the leaders of the Neckwear Workers' Union strike that started on July 4.

On an evening in July, 1906, right after Pine was elected Secretary of the U. H. T., he was walking along Rutgers Street and saw a crowd. On the sidewalk was a man who had been badly injured by an explosion of a seltzer bottle in a cellar factory. Pine and others helped him to the drug store, telephoned for an ambulance and the worker was taken to the hospital.

The next morning Pine began to organize all seltzer factory workers on the East Side. Seltzer factories were then in dark cellars and the workers slaved 70-80 hours per week, and many of them slept in these factory cellars. Before dawn they began to fill the seltzer bottles so that the drivers could pick them up at 7 A. M. They earned from $4.00 to $5.00 a week. There was always the danger of bottle explosion from which many workers died.

Soon, as a result of Pine's activity, all these workers were in a union. Just as soon as it became known that the union was a fact, the bosses ordered a lockout. The union countered with a strike call. The strike lasted 24 weeks. Pine arranged for other unions and other workers to help these embattled and hungry strikers. He then helped organize the workers into a cooperative shop in real competition with the bosses. The fear of this cooperative competition caused the bosses to yield and then the strike was settled.

The union joined others in successfully pushing for legislation for better working conditions, abolishing these cellar factories and safeguarding the workers against explosions and other hazards.

In 1907 Pine helped organize the cloakmaker strike. He went from shop meeting to shop meeting. Coming to a cloakmaker mass meeting at Manhattan Lyceum on 4th Street, he saw the workers outside the hall, due to the fact that these officers of the union did not have enough money to pay the $25.00 rental for the meeting hall. Pine, too, didn't have enough money but he had a gold watch and went directly to Lombard's, the pawn-broker, pawned the watch, paid for the meeting hall and the meeting was held.

The year 1909 was one of great significance to the Jewish Labor movement. First, there was held the great Baker Strike of 20,000 workers. Pine helped to organize the strike and was the general who successfully concluded it after two hard months of struggle. This Baker victory was like the appearance of a swallow which indicated signs of spring in the Jewish Labor movement. On July 2, 1909, there was held the great Baker Victory Demonstration at the conclusion of which Pine announced that since he obtained excellent results in looking out for the welfare of the Jewish laboring masses, he was resigning from the leadership of the U. H. T. and would go into the printing business and would now look out for the welfare of his own family.

Despite his disassociation with the U. H. T. in an official capacity, Pine and Samuel Schindler, the Secretary-Treasurer of the Waistmakers' Union, helped organize the first general strike of the waistmakers which started on November 22, 1909.

In the evening of the 21st, when the strike was declared, ten large mass meetings were held and Pine was among the speakers at most of them along with Jacob Panken, Meyer London, Bernard Weinstein, Rose Schniederman and others. Eighteen thousand strikers, mostly women and children, were called out. The bitter struggle lasted 16 weeks till March 12, 1910, when it was successfully concluded. During the strike another 12,000 joined the union which won a 54 hour week and 15 to 20% increase in wages. These 30,000 Ladies Waist Maker Union members thus strengthened the then weak I. L. G. W. U., of which it was a part.

The next great effort to win rights for Jewish labor was the great Cloakmakers' strike in which were joined the Shirtmakers, Raincoat Makers and Department Store Alteration workers—in all, 70,000 ladies' garment workers. The strike was called July 7, 1910. The shop meetings were addressed mostly by Socialists; Abraham Cahan, Morris Hilquitt, Meyer London, B. Feigenbaum, Max Pine, Jacob Panken, Benjamin Schlesinger, A. I. Shiplakoff and others. The strike was settled on September 2, 1910, with the assistance of Louis D. Brandeis and Louis Marshall. The "Protocol" agreement was signed providing, among other things for a settlement of disputes, ten paid holidays yearly and the "Preferential" shop (a shop in which union conditions were to be maintained and union men given preference on hiring).

It was the success of this strike which gave the impetus to the organization of the Tailor Strike in 1912 in which Pine did the impossible. He organized 130,000 tailors and that strike finally put Jewish Labor in the vanguard of national labor unionism.

A milestone in the struggle for better conditions of labor was the catastrophic Triangle factory fire which broke out on Saturday, March 25, 1911, at 4:30 P. M. The three upper stories of the ten-story factory building at 23 Washington Place, where the Triangle Waist Company had its factory became an inferno and 146 persons, mostly woman and girls, lost their lives. Nearly 50 were killed when, terror-stricken, they leaped from the high windows; 50 were burned to death and the rest died of suffocation or were trampled to death. Much of the great loss in this most horrifying factory fire till then to occur in the U. S. was due to locked doors.

That same day the U. H. T. met at Forward Hall and demanded better conditions of work and threatened strikes to attain them. At that meeting the following resolution was adopted: "That all unions should work for the safety of their workers and when bosses refuse to help, they should strike against them." Ten delegates from the ladies' waist-makers' union appeared at that meeting and urged that the unrecognized bodies of the workers be buried with a labor demonstration.

Pine, Weinstein and Joseph Goldstein were designated to draw up the "Call to Action." A committee with Pine and Weinstein as leaders was organized to gather funds to help those unfortunates who remained alive, to help families of the unfortunate dead and to pay for the burial of the recognizable dead.

A great funeral demonstration was organized by Pine and Weinstein and held on Wednesday, April 5th, when in a severe rainstorm, 120,000 workers marched from Clinton Hall, the headquarters of the Waist Makers' Union, to Washington Place, the scene of the fire. Over one-half million people viewed the demonstration.

The sum of $16,000—then a large sum—was raised by the Pine Committee and turned over to the Red Cross to help the sufferers. The Forward, too, set up a fund to help. It also turned over its money to the Red Cross, which, through its own sources, raised and distributed an additional $120,000.

Although the New York State Factory Inspection Act was on the books since 1886, the factory regulations were very meager and almost inconsequential. It took the Triangle Fire to awaken the community to demand and obtain strict requirements of factory conditions. Governor Dix of New York State appointed the New York State Factory Investigating Commission. As a result, State laws and City ordinances were passed putting teeth in the respective hands of the State Labor Department and of the City Health Department.

The idea of working women and children in shops pained Pine particularly. He worked for laws to restrict their work and improve their working conditions. In 1907 the New York Statute prohibiting night work for women was declared unconstitutional by the Court of Appeals on the ground that it was an unwarranted interference with the right to freedom of contract. Finally, a change in thinking took place and the 1913 law was declared constitutional in 1915.

The most important cases favoring laws for female workers are the Oregon Laundry case before the U. S. Supreme Court in 1908 upholding a ten-hour law for women workers and the Ritche case before the Illinois Supreme Court in 1910 upholding a similar law. It is interesting to note that Louis D. Brandeis, later Supreme Court Justice, wrote the briefs on behalf of labor in both cases.

Pine's concern for abolishing child labor is best illustrated by the following excerpts from an address he delivered at the Forty-Second Annual Convention of the American Federation of Labor at Cincinnati, Ohio, in June, 1922:

" . . . whoever makes children work, whether it be a rude contractor or a refined gentleman, he is nothing short of a criminal and an enemy to mankind. The children are the seeds of the country, the seeds by which a country lives, grows, survives and succeeds. We have in our State (New York) and I believe in other states, laws that forbid fishing out of season, that forbid killing game out of season. Why not have a law to forbid killing and crippling children out of season?

"And pray, brothers and sisters, is there any necessity for taking children out of schools and sending them into factories? . . . it is natural that you men of labor should take up the case of the children and defend them, because it is your children and the children of our fellow working men who will be in the factories. The children of the rich will be exempt, as a rule.

" . . . I will conclude by asking the privilege to be permitted in this fight to help free the children, to help free the workers, because the freedom of the workers is the freedom of mankind."

Child labor has greatly troubled our labor leaders. The Constitution of the United States was silent on the question of restricting child labor. Some states, the enlightened ones, passed laws to restrict child labor. However, most of the states were laggard in this respect. After much urging by labor leaders, the U. S. Congress finally passed the 1916 Child Labor Law, which excluded from interstate commerce products of factories employing children under fourteen years of age. However, in 1918 the U. S. Supreme Court declared the law unconstitutional. Congress then tried another tack and passed another Child Labor Law which imposed a tax of 10% on the net profits of factories employing children under the age of fourteen. This law, too, was declared unconstitutional.

It was just after the latter decision that the said A. F. of L. Convention took place at Cincinnati, where Pine made the foregoing statement about child labor.

Immediately proposals were made for a constitutional amendment. The Sixty-eighth Congress passed a Child Labor Amendment by a Joint Resolution which was passed by the House on April 26, 1924 by a vote of 297 to 69 and by the Senate on June 2, 1924, by a vote of 61 to 23. The said proposed amendment reads:

"Sec. 1: The Congress shall have power to limit, regulate and prohibit the labor of persons under eighteen years of age.

"Sec. 2: The power of the several States is unimpaired by this article except that the operation of State Laws shall be suspended to the extent necessary to give effect to legislation enacted by the Congress."

Twenty-eight states have already ratified it and thirty-six are necessary to make it into law. It is noteworthy that thirty-two years have already elapsed since Congress passed the proposed amendment and there is still a long way to go before it can become law. It is to be noted too that New York, one of the enlightened states which has its own Child Labor Laws has until now failed to ratify the said Child Labor Amendment. The principal objection to the amendment is made by a religious group which fears that the words regulate labor of persons under 18 may be interpreted as a regulation of religious practices.

Pine continued to work for the improvement of the lot of the worker. Even as late as 1912 workers earned starvation wages. In a Pennsylvania textile mill dispute, Rabbi Stephen S. Wise was appointed a mediator between employer and employes and reported that the weekly salary for winders, doublers, reelers, lacers, spinners, etc., was $4.75 per week. A worker in the paper box industry in New York City received $6.00 per week. Much work had to be done.

Pine also helped in the Fur Strike of 1912 which was begun on July 12, 1912 and successfully ended on September 8, 1912.

All of this labor activity was laying the groundwork for the great Tailor Strike called December 31, 1912, which was the crowning glory of Pine's service to the Jewish workers and had a substantial impact on the entire American Labor Movement.

Chapter 7

UNITED HEBREW TRADES

The United Hebrew Trades was the center of all Jewish union activities. It helped the individual immigrants as well as their unions in their struggle for a better life and better conditions. In fact, the very existence of many unions is due in large measure to the work of the United Hebrew Trades.

The value of the U. H. T. is very well described by William Green, the President of the A. F. of L., in his message called "Organized Labor; The Only Bulwark of Freedom," as follows: ". . . It would be a good deal less than the truth to say merely that the U. H. T. as an organization helped the Jewish masses. It has done a great deal more than that. It has contributed in large measure to the welfare of the entire organized labor movement in the United States. I want to discuss in a broader sense the debt that organized labor in this country owes to the Jews. It is especially fitting at this time that this deep obligation should be emphasized and clarified.

"The Jew who came here towards the end of the last century was shocked to find economic oppression in the land of promise. Where they had been led to expect streets paved with gold and silver, they found squalor, hunger and sweat shops. As victims of oppression in other lands, they naturally were stirred by economic injustice. They looked around for a solution. They attended labor meetings. They learned about labor unions, and they enlisted as enthusiastic soldiers in organized Labor's fight to improve the conditions of American workers."

Praise of the leadership of the U. H. T. is unbounded.
David Dubinsky, the President of the International Ladies
Garment Workers' Union, used the following language:

"When Morris Feinstone stepped, twenty years
ago, into the office of Associate Secretary of the
U. H. T., he found in it a tradition of leadership
of the highest calibre. Men of the type of Max
Pine and Abraham Shiplakoff had occupied the
post before, men who left an indelible mark in the
chronicle of organized labor among the immigrant
working masses in this country."

Samuel Schor, a Vice-President of the I.L.G.W.U. describes the effect of the U. H. T. and its leaders on the
Jewish Labor movement thus:

"Today we can not only help ourselves but help
others.

"We lived through a period when we had to de-
pend upon the charity of others. Not only our
unions, but the unions of the men's clothing industry and others lived through a period when
the U. H. T. was father and mother to us, in a
period when soup kitchens were established for
hungry pickets and for the distribution of food
packages to workers' wives and children, a period
when Weinstein, Shiplakoff and Pine carried on
their shoulders the entire weight of the Jewish
Labor movement."

The U. H. T. was a product of the Socialist movement.
Jacob Magidoff was the creator of the idea of a U. H. T.
Magidoff admitted that he copied the idea from the United
German Trades but with one significant difference. The
Germans first organized unions and when there existed a
large number of unions, they were united in the United
German Trades. Magidoff and his Socialists decided to

organize a United Hebrew Trades to help organize unions. It was Magidoff who made the motion at a meeting of Branch 8 of the Socialist Labor Party to organize the U. H. T. The motion was enthusiastically received and unanimously adopted. A committee consisting of J. Magidoff, Bernard Weinstein and J. Lederman was appointed for the purpose of preparing plans for its organization.

The committee met at Magidoff's home at 189 Madison Street, discussed the problem and decided to issue a call for a conference of organization. The response was electric. The Russian Jews, who came here in the 80's after the Russian pogroms, were filled with revolutionary ideals and with vim, vigor and a burning zeal threw themselves into the struggle for the freedom of the working class.

The conference was held on October 9, 1886 at the Socialist Labor Lyceum at 25 East 4 Street. Attending the conference were: Morris Hilquitt, L. Bandes, J. Magidoff and Bernard Weinstein, representing Branch 8 of the Socialist Labor Party; M. Weber, the Hebrew Typesettters' Union; I. Krinsky and L. Lentzer, the Hebrew Choristers' Union, M. Sinonoff, the Hebrew Actors' Union, M. Geriche of the United Hebrew Trade and W. Rosenberg of the German Socialist Publication. Bernard Weinstein was elected Secretary and Morris Hilquitt Corresponding Secretary. The United Hebrew Trades was then and there born. Unions with a total membership of 70 were then represented in the U. H. T.

A three point program was adopted. (1) Mutual assistance among its unions. (2) aid to existing unions outside its rank and organization of new ones as quickly as possible; and (3) spread of Socialist doctrine among the workers.

The U. H. T. immediately commenced its work and added a fourth point: Americanization. There soon developed among the Jewish immigrant masses a love for the country of their adoption. But for a mere accident of chance, these workers might have remained in Europe and been the victims of the Nazis.

It was not easy to improve the conditions of the workers because there was resistance all around. First, there were the sweat shop bosses; then many immigrants themselves were timid for fear of loss of jobs; then there was the suspicion of the American worker toward the foreign born who, they feared, would undermine their positions. In addition to all of the above, Jewish immigrants had no traditions for cooperative action in the form of unions like those developed in America, which had culminated in the American Federation of Labor.

However, relations changed. These Jewish unions became cooperative and friendly and joined the A. F. of L., and helped shape American labor policy. They became the backbone of the progressive American Labor movement and set standards and examples of how labor and management and capital can work together in peace and harmony for the benefit of all. The I. L. G. W. U., the Amalgamated Clothing Workers Union and the Millinery Union are leaders in the field.

The first real attempts of the U. H. T. to organize a union were made among the cloakmakers. Bernard Weinstein sent Joseph Barondess, who was a member of Branch 8 of the S. L. P., to organize the cloakmakers. After some preliminary work, a strike was called. Barondess slept at the strike headquarters at 92 Hester Street. The strike was settled on July 23, 1890 victoriously, with Barondess acting as chairman of the committee to work out the settlement.

The bosses left no stones unturned in their effort to destroy the unions and their leaders. An epoch-making incident was the arrest and imprisonment of Joseph Barondess.

As an aftermath of the 1890 strike, Barondess charged that the cloak shop of Popkin & Marks, leading New York

City manufacturers, had broken the settlement agreement. The employers denied any violation and refused to arbitrate. Barondess then struck the shop. On February 9, 1891, he reached an agreement to settle the strike, but as a condition of settlement, Barondess asked for $500. to pay the strikers for lost time before he would permit the strikers to return to work. After some negotiations the firm gave Barondess a check for an agreed sum of $100. made payable to him personally.

Barondess personally cashed the check and turned the money over to the union to be distributed among the strikers. He then declared the strike at an end and ordered the strikers to return to work. He was at that time the manager of the cloakmakers' union.

Soon, on complaint of the bosses, Barondess was arrested and indicted for extortion. He was tried and convicted. His conviction was reversed by the General Term. The General Term decision was then reversed and the conviction reinstated by a 4 to 3 vote by the Court of Appeals. Barondess lingered in jail. Finally, Pine succeeded in organizing an appeal to Governor Fowler and Barondess was pardoned. Barondess had to sit in jail several times for no reason other than that he was a union leader and the police and courts were doing the bidding of the bosses.

The shirt, pants, suspender, soda water and kneepants makers were organized, but the going was difficult. The press, police, courts, schools and other social groups regarded unions as dangerous. Distribution of leaflets was almost impossible. When a few handbills would be dropped, the union members would be arrested for violating a sanitary ordinance.

The United Hebrew Trades took steps to break through the opposition. Shop strikes developed but union strikes were many times still-born. The U. H. T. set out to raise funds which were so desperately needed to carry on union activities. Money was needed to organize mass meetings, set up union headquarters, support strikers' children, give rent to strikers' families, give them food or pay for their burial.

In addition to the opposition from the outside, the United Hebrew Trades had internal opposition. Daniel DeLeon, about whom we shall write at length in a later chapter, wanted political domination of the unions by the Socialist Labor Party. Most of the U. H. T. representatives insisted upon freedom for the U. H. T. from political domination. The inner stuggle was long for it was not until 1897, when the real break came and the DeLeonites expelled the leaders of the U. H. T. from the Publishing Company of the S. L. P. and the founding of the "Forward," that the U. H. T. was really freed from political domination. Though it professed itself Socialist in sympathy and out-look, its members could hold any political views.

The U. H. T. thus adopted the Gompers political principal of rewarding friends and punishing enemies of labor. It is interesting to note that that philosophy guided the A. F. of L. and C. I. O. except for the 1952 presidential election.

The U. H. T. was like a little "United Nations" with immigrant Jews, Hungarians, Swedes, Italians, Germans, Russians, and "native" Americans as members. The tie between all was a practical one; improving working conditions, strengthening their collective bargaining powers, removing the fears of exploitation through strong organization and increasing cultural opportunities through increasing economic opportunities.

In 1906 Max Pine was elected Secretary and Executive Director of the U. H. T. He at once threw himself in the campaign for strengthening the U. H. T. and the unions. Some of his union activities have heretofore been described.

At the time of his election the U. H. T. had 26 unions as members. As a result of his activities the U. H. T. was strengthened so that when he resigned in July, 1909, to enter private printing business, the U. H. T. had 41 unions as members.

During his incumbency in office, America went through its 1907 financial crisis which greatly affected the poor immigrant workers. Pine had to retain what had already been won and to organize others for the U. H. T. His principal headache was to take care of the numberless dispossess cases.

In 1914 the U. H. T. designated Pine as a delegate to the International Socialist Congress that was scheduled to be convened in Vienna. He embarked on the Aquitania for London, and upon arrival World War I was declared and Pine was stranded in London. After being the Guest of Honor at a great London Trade Union Banquet, he sailed for America in a convoy which took 17 days to reach the United States.

In that same year there took place the struggle between the U. H. T. and the A. F. L. At the Philadelphia convention the A. F. of L. refused to recognize the new Amalgamated Clothing Workers that was formed as the result of the great Tailor strike outlined in an earlier chapter.

Daniel J. Tobin of the Teamsters' Union demanded to know why the U. H. T. was organized. Samuel Gompers of the A. F. of L. stated:

> "In Russia and Poland Jewish people were subjected to indignities, injustices and cruelties. They had to leave their countries. Great masses came to the U. S."

James Duncan remarked:

> "When they arrived some jealousy was aroused in New York and they were forbidden member-

ship in some unions. They sought shelter and organized themselves until they could prove loyalty and faithfulness to the trade union movement in America. The vicious employers took advantage of them and the immigrants found themselves helpless because of their greed. Since some unions refused them membership, they formed Yiddish speaking groups. The movement grew. It was tolerated and did splendid work. The U. H. T. is a transitory, not a permanent body."

The A. F. of L. adopted a resolution requesting the International unions to direct their locals in New York to withdraw from the U. H. T. unless it expelled the tailor local unions. The U. H. T. refused to do so despite the fact that Gompers appeared personally at a U. H. T. meeting. Thereafter there was no further cooperation from the A. F. of L.

It is interesting to note that Duncan's prognostigation about the transitory existence of the U. H. T. was proved to be correct. Whereas in the early days the U. H. T. carried on all the union activities for the unions, even carried on their strikes, eventually, the unions, with the aid of the U. H. T., became stronger. As the unions developed and grew large and strong, the functions of the U. H. T. were taken over by the unions themselves. Only the small unions remain in the U. H. T. for they still need help. The I. L. G. W. U., the Amalgamated Clothing Workers' Union, the Millinery Union, etc. no longer need help from the U. H. T. In effect, these unions help the U. H. T. carry on in a limited sphere. Its functions are principally the following: helping the smaller unions get better working conditions and higher wages; publicizing the appeal for public support of their demands; appealing for the union label; making public the unfairness of police and the courts, when they are unfair; acting as liason between the Jewish labor movement and the A. F. of L. and C. I. O.; conducting an immigration bureau to help find work for new arrivals; having an amnesty committee to work for freedom of political prisoners.

In 1916 Pine was re-elected Secretary and Director of the U. H. T. and held that post until 1925.

The U. H. T. took an active interest in the trials of Moyer, Haywood & Pettibone. It sent money, agitated, publicized and awoke public opinion. The same was done for Tom Mooney, Sacco & Vanzetti, and many other labor and political prisoners.

In 1920 the suitcase workers' union had a strike which lasted six months. Their leaders were arrested and imprisoned. Pine was instrumental in freeing them after several months of hard and energetic work.

The U. H. T. was also the mainstay of the People's Relief Committee for Aid of War Victims abroad during and after World War I. More about that in another chapter.

A great deal is heard and written about the internal struggle in the American Labor unions caused by the Communists in their unions. The I. L. G. W. U. recently went through a bitter struggle and the Communists were overwhelmingly defeated.

The struggle with the Communists started right after the Russian Revolution. With the birth of Communism in the U. S. A., the Communists tried to take control of the unions by boring from within.

Pine was a leading antagonist and fought the Communists at every step. Pine described the struggle. He stated that they (the Communists) spread lies and false accusations against the labor leaders of the unions, and that they befuddled the minds of the workers. The U. H. T. recognized their aims and warned the workers.

The minutes of the U. H. T. for October 31, 1921 under the signature of Max Pine, the Secretary, reads:

"There was read to the meeting an invitation from the Communists, who issue a weekly, 'Emes' (Truth). They are calling a conference for the purpose of publishing a daily. During the debate, it was shown that these 'Truth' people have been spreading untruths about the unions. It is unanimously decided to refuse the invitation to the conference and also to issue a public declaration why the U. H. T. will have nothing to do with them."

Several excerpts characteristic of the entire declaration, written by Max Pine, are as follows:

"For the past few years the labor movement lived through a time that required great effort on behalf of the U. H. T. Unions had great difficulty in calling strikes against large and small employers who took advantage of the dark clouds of the reactionaries and who attacked our unions with merciless and indescribable fury.

"During such periods, the so-called 'Saviors of the Proletariat,' those who want to bring down the Messiah by force, lost no oportunity to attack with poison the most important figures in the labor movement. In their weekly, formerly called 'Kampf' (Strife) and now 'Emes' (Truth), they never wrote one bad word against those who exploit the workers.

"With arrogance—which correctly characterizes this group—they set out on a campaign to destroy the confidence of the workers in their unions."

The declaration goes on to give a bill of particulars of the instances of intrigue and terror which the Communists used and ends with a call to the workers not to take part in the conference.

Pine was personally and bitterly attacked by the Communists. He weathered the storm and so presented his case to the laboring masses that his views were accepted by the union workers. For a period of about a year the Communists did take control of the I. L. G. W. U. but they were eventually ousted from office, and have not been able to gain mastery to this very day.

Chapter 8

SOCIALISM

Socialism was the driving force that enabled most of the Jewish labor leaders to persevere in the face of the tremendous obstacles to their organizing the immigrant laborer. Pine became a deeply sincere Socialist after his arrival here in 1890. He came to Socialism not through books but from want, suffering, exploitation and hard labor.

The unsuccessful Revolution of 1848 in Germany laid the groundwork for the beginnings of Socialism in the United States. Many leaders of the revolution came to the United States and soon there was organized the United German Trades, after which the United Hebrew Trades was copied.

In 1864 Karl Marx founded the First International Socialist Congress. Immediately the Socialists began to function in New York, Illinois and elsewhere "under leaders who could scarcely speak the English language." The meetings—the first of which was held in New York City in 1867—were conducted in German; those present sang German songs; the official organ of the party was "The Socialist," published in German at the Labor Lyceum.

In the summer of 1889 there was assembled in Paris the Second International Socialist Congress. Busche, who was the editor of the "Workman's Advocate," published in New York, was a delegate to that Congress. Upon his return a struggle broke out in the publication association. "The Socialist," under the editorship of W. Rosenberg, a radical German Socialist, attacked the non-Socialist unions. The "Volks Zeitung," also in German, under the editorship of Sergei Schevitch and later under Alexander Jonas, two leaders of the Socialist Labor Party, opposed the attack. The latter two wanted the unions to be with them, near to them so as to teach the workers Socialism. The others wanted to destroy the unions. The "Workman's Advo-cate," then controlled by the National Executive of the Socialist Labor Party, sided with The Socialist.

DANIEL DeLEON was then just coming into his own as the leader of the Socialist Labor Party and soon became the leader of all Socialist thinking in the United States until the advent of Eugene V. Debs in the late '90s. DeLeon had been greatly influenced by the Henry George campaign for Mayor of New York in 1886. He sided with those who wanted to subordinate the unions to the party and the unions who refused to follow the Socialist line had to be destroyed. DeLeon's group was called the Lassalean Socialist group. The others, the Jonas Schevitch group, which held that trade unions must develop power and organize before the Socialist Revolution could hope to remedy the ills of society, was called the Marxist group. Pine soon became one of the leaders of the latter group.

JOHANN MOST was the leader of the then powerful group of Anarchists, also a German product. He was a great orator and preached "powder and lead to free the world." On one occasion he walked on the stage with a gun and announced, "It was the only way to get results." He circulated a pamphlet on how to make bombs and was imprisoned many times. The Anarchists published the German weekly "Freiheit". Their headquarters was at Schwab's saloon on First Street, New York City.

Johann Most fiercely fought the Socialists—social democrats—for taking part in political campaigns. His chief assistant was one Braunschweig, a furniture worker and union leader. Most stated that with 500 Braunschweigs he could bring about the American Revolution.

Socialism was introduced to Yiddish-speaking workers by Abraham Cahan. At a Socialist meeting held in Golden Hall on Rivingston Street on July 27, 1882, Morovitch, the Chairman, who spoke in Russian, introduced Sergei Schevitch, who also spoke in Russian, on the theme "The Last

Pogroms in Russia and Socialism." During the discussion period which followed, Abraham Cahan spoke from the floor, also in Russian. But his plea was to propagandize among the Yiddish workers not in German or Russian but in Yiddish, the language they understood.

Soon thereafter, in a celler on Sixth Street, frequented by Anarchists, Cahan delivered the first Socialist speech in Yiddish on the theme "Socialism and the Teachings of Karl Marx." Thereafter in 1884 there was organized the Russian Jewish Workers Alliance for the purpose of spreading Socialist thought in Yiddish.

At the First Congress of Central Labor Unions of New York, May 1, 1886 was proclaimed the International Workers Holiday and on that date the first May Day Labor parade took place in New York City. Thirty thousand workers marched and held a demonstration at Union Square. Magidoff, a political writer, states that there were sixty thousand marchers.

The principal speaker was Henry George, the liberal, economist, reformer and Single Taxer, who, that year became the candidate for Mayor of New York on the United Labor Party ticket. Samuel Gompers, then president of the American Federation of Labor, and Schevitch also spoke at the May Day demonstration.

The Russian Jewish Workers Alliance was split in 1886 over the controversy of the place of politics in trade unions. One group under the leadership of Yanofsky and Zolotaroff joined the Anarchists and the others under the leadership of Cahan and M. Zametkin organized Branch 8 of the Socialist Labor Party. This latter group included the first Yiddish agitators for unionization in America. It included Cahan, Zametkin, Miller, Hilquitt and Barondess. Pine joined this group after his arrival in 1890.

Chicago was then the center of the movement for shorter hours of labor. In 1886 police attacked a workers' demonstration and killed seven workers. Thereupon a bomb was thrown at Haymarket Square killing seven policemen. Seven Anarchist leaders were arrested, tried, convicted of murder and sentenced to be hanged. Four were executed on November 11, 1887, one committed suicide in jail and two had their sentences commuted to life imprisonment. Later, Governor John P. Altgeld held that the convictions were fraudulent, unjust and issued a pardon.

On the eve of the executions in Chicago, there was held a huge demonstration march on Fifth Avenue, New York City, in which the Social Democrats joined. Many Anarchists came armed with weapons and bombs. The police in the streets, hallways, buildings and roofs were waiting for the trouble they expected from the Anarchists, and the Anarchists were waiting for the police to start the trouble. There was plenty of tension and excitement but no trouble. Neither side dared to begin and nothing happened.

Early in 1889 the Anarchists held a convention at the Essex Market Armory to which they invited all Jewish radicals, Anarchists, Social Democrats, unions and educational institutions. On the fourth day of the convention a split took place and the Social Democrats and their unions left the hall. They then organized "The Arbeiter Zeitung Publishing Association" for the purpose of publishing the Yiddish weekly, "Die Arbeiter Zeitung." In two months they raised several thousand dollars and brought Philip Kranz, a leading British Socialist from London to New York, and made him editor. Morris Hilquitt was elected manager of the new weekly at $7.00 per week. The weekly first appeared on March 7, 1890.

Those who remained in the convention hall, principally the Anarchists, decided to publish also in Yiddish, "Die Freie Arbeiter Shtime," which first appeared on July 4th, 1890.

These two groups and their respective magazines kept up constant discussions of the rights of labor and the place of unions in the Socialist and political movements. The question at all Socialist meetings was how to carry on oral and written propaganda for Socialism and the tactics to be used in winning over the trade unions.

The Yiddish Socialists' meeting at the Jewish Socialist Labor Lyceum at 91 Delancey Street in July, 1891, determined also to publish their own Yiddish monthly called "Zukunft" and the first issue appeared in January, 1892.

The Independent United Labor Party which ran Henry George for Mayor of New York in 1886 was an unholy alliance of liberals, reformers, radicals, Socialists of all shades of thinking and beliefs, and Anarchists. That type of alliance could not long exist. Soon the split came and the party was liquidated.

DeLeon thereupon joined the Socialist Labor Party. He was a man of iron character. Once a decision was made he pushed right through to the goal. Soon after joining the S. L. P., which was then in German hands, he set out to unseat the controlling Germans. He seized power and ruled with an iron hand. He was a real despot and brooked no opposition and permitted no free speech. He was a real political "boss" in the worst sense of the term. He was called "dictator" by the Social Democrats.

He was the chief of the "clique" that ran the "Arbeiter Zeitung Publishing Society" and that group bored from within to destroy the prevailing existing unions.

Of interest, as Pine stated it, is the fact that the DeLeonites hated the Social Democrats more than the reactionary exploiters of labor. This situation is now being repeated when the Communists hate the Social Democrats more than they hate the capitalists, and would prefer to destroy the Social Democratic unions in the International Ladies Garment Workers Union, the Amalgamated Clothing Workers and the International Millinery and Hatters Union

before they attack the reactionary capitalists. In the
I. L. G. W. U. triannual local elections of 1950, the Communists were overwhelmingly beaten after a bitter campaign.

The reason for such hatreds can be found in the psycho-
logical analysis of the feelings of rivals. Each rival would
like first to destroy his first immediate rival before he
attempts to attack the others.

DeLeon believed that mankind was divided into two
classes: Socialists and Fakirs; there was no middle element. He was too many times insulting. Alexander Jonas
once asked him that if all non-Socialists were fakirs, where
would he get the people for the Social Revolution? DeLeon
answered that Jonas, the great Socialist leader, didn't
understand intellectual Socialism; that he was an igno-
ramus. Jonas countered: "But we hope to recruit new
followers for our ideals not only from the ranks of labor
but from all other parties and it is for that that we carry
on such great propaganda. Therefore, why must we con-
demn the whole world?" DeLeon made his characteristic
grimace, twisted his lips and shot a glance from his sharp
but youthful eye and turned away, and did not answer.

In debates he insulted all opponents. Once he yelled
at his opponent: "The trouble with you, why you don't
understand, is that you have cockroaches in your head."

In his daily, "People", edited by him in English for the
S. L. P. as its official organ, he used to insult those who
asked questions. His writing contained numerous anti-
Semitic diatribes. He called Morris Wintchefsky, Went-
chester. DeLeon hated him. Henry Slobodin he called
Slobodinofsky. Despite his fanaticism and despotism,
DeLeon was a remarkable personality—a brilliant orator
and writer with a sharp pen and a remarkable memory. It
is no wonder that he was the guiding spirit of the Socialist
movement until Debs came on the scene.

The "Genossen" of the "Arbeiter Zeitung Publishing Association" stuck to him like flies to honey. They defied him and followed him to extremes wherever he went. They followed him in his desire to defeat the leaders of the "Knights of Labor" in 1895. The Jewish unions left that order, for when he organized the Socialist Trade and Labor Alliance by "hook or crook" the Jewish unions had to join.

Many Jewish Socialists opposed his dictatorship, but he fought his opposition with all his might. In his paper he made fun of and insulted Cahan, Miller, Pine and others. These people held the leadership in the opposition to the S. L. P. control of the Publishing Association. At a caucus meeting of the opposition they decided to gain control by proposing thirty new members to the Association. The meeting of the Publishing Association was held on January 7, 1897, at 73 Ludlow Street.

Joseph Schlossberg was then secretary of the Publishing Association. He was a DeLeonite. Pine was one of the opposition who was refused admission to the meeting.

Pine described the meeting in the 25th Jubilee issue of the "Forward" thus:

"I was one of the opposition and was kept out. I banged on the door and was refused admission. They opened the door, saw me and closed it again. Then I tried to push in the door but without success. Then I asked those behind me to push and we broke down the door. A tumult ensued; in fact, some fighting took place.

"On that night of January 7, 1897, there was born the 'Forward.' On that night there took place the split in the Jewish Socialist movement and there was thus signalled the beginning of the end of the S. L. P., of DeLeon's daily, 'The People,' of the Jewish Socialist daily, 'Der Abend Blatt' (Evening News), of its tactics to break unions, of its dictatorship by the clique over the masses of workers and Socialists.

"As the opposition saw that they could accomplish nothing with the cards stacked against them by the DeLeonites, one of the opposition yelled out, 'Genossen, Kumt' (Let's go). Fifty-two members of the Arbeiter Zeitung Publishing Association left the hall in a body. Among those who left were Cahan, Miller, Wintchefsky, Zametkin and Pine. It is interesting to note that Hilquitt and Kranz, though opposed to DeLeon, did not join the revolt and did not leave. Of course, neither did Schlossberg, who sided with DeLeon."

When these fifty-two left the hall, they were met by a large group of friends and sympathizers who waited many hours in the biting cold for the result of that meeting. Those who left the meeting were greeted warmly and enthusiastically. Someone had arranged for a meeting hall in the Valhalla basement. The meeting hall was to be used by a society whose secretary was the one who arranged for the hall. He had written the members of his society that there would be no meeting that night, and so reserved the hall for the said oppositionists who went there directly.

A new meeting was held. Speaker after speaker repeated the sins that the leadership of the S. L. P. and its press committee committed against them and labor in general. It was past midnight when they really started to function. They organized themselves into a press association. Its purpose was to publish a Yiddish daily. They decided to issue a public statement as to why they left the Arbeiter Zeitung Publishing Association. Louis Miller volunteered to write it. A roll call was taken and all of the fifty-two who left the Arbeiter Zeitung agreed to join the new association.

The Miller declaration took the form of a pamphlet which was widely distributed. However, it was too strong in language. Miller used expressions that were not in order and many of the said fifty-two would have refused to publicize it. But it was too late. It had already been publicized. Miller wrote the entire thing himself. Some of the complaints were: it stated that some unsavory figures gained control of the movement; that "loyal" members of the association expelled the most active members of the movement by trickery so that those remaining could control the movement without opposition; that the loyalties built up a Jewish Tammany machine and armed it with filthy ammunition in order to keep their jobs. Pine and others were very dissatisfied with the pamphlet and felt badly about it. The energetic Miller later stated that he purposely used such language and expressions in order to burn all bridges behind them so that none would return to the old association.

Pine and his associates swallowed the expressions with dissatisfaction but without much protest. Only Henry King published a protest in the Evening News. But he, too, did not return to the association. The loyaltists defended themselves and issued replies and set forth the reasons for the opposition as they saw it.

At that January 7th meeting, there was decided to call a convention of all Socialists, party districts, unions and all other organizations that spoke Yiddish and that agreed with the Socialist philosophy of the class struggle.

That convention was held at Valhalla Hall on January 30, and 31, 1897. It was a great success. Delegates were there from New York, Philadelphia, Boston, New Haven, Hartford and nearly all Jewish unions including those that belonged to the United Garment Workers. In all, 73 organizations were represented.

In order to prove to the world that they merely opposed the Jewish Genossen of the Arbeiter Zeitung Publishing

Association and not the Socialist Labor Party, and to show that they really wanted to improve the party and not to fight it, they first adopted the following declaration:

"We declare that only those who are active and faithful to the platform of the Socialist Labor Party should participate."

They also adopted a resolution of purpose:

"To hold high the flag of the International class struggle and to work with all our might for the Socialist Labor party."

The convention then issued concrete demands: a free press; all important party and union problems should be discussed in the daily Socialist paper; the Socialist press should not be controlled by a voluntary association but by representatives of the masses, by delegates.

These demands broke the walls of the "loyalist" fortress. They also demonstrated and proved that DeLeon, claiming a desire to build Socialist unions, actually created civil war in the unions, ruined the workers' economy, made the workers poorer than before. It is important to note that DeLeon did not organize an opposition to the Longshoremen's and Railway unions, which were not Socialistic, but did organize opposition unions to the capmakers and the cloakmakers which were really Socialistic.

These Socialists were poor but they worked with a will, determination, spirit, enthusiasm and energy. They were so poor they didn't have enough money for a banquet for the delegates, though food was very cheap. They could only afford a dairy dinner at fifty cents per person in the Valhalla sub-cellar. The tables were unwashed, the walls had spider webs; bare tables were placed on wooden horses; the meal consisted of herring, bread and kashe (groats). Many of the delegates did not attend the banquet for they could not afford even the fifty cents.

Despite being so poor, they decided to publish a daily.

Spring arrived. Their headquarters was in Corlears Hook Park at the foot of Jackson Street. There they met every night, discussed matters and collected pennies, nickels, dimes and quarters. Two young lads would race across the Park. Bets were made as to who would win and the winnings went to the contemplated "Forward," named after the Socialist Party organ in Germany. Most of the fines collected by unions were turned over to the publishing committee.

When they collected $1,000, a great deal of money at the time, they decided to hold three out-of-town mass-meetings at Philadelphia, Boston and Hartford. It turned out that all the meetings were failures. In addition to not showing any profit, the leaders actually lost the $1,000 they had and were forced to borrow money for the return fare of the speakers, including Pine, who had spoken at each meeting.

At the New York meeting following the fiascos, an ash-colored, tiny capmaker walked toward the platform and laid $25 on the chairman's table. When the chairman announced the said first donation, there was a rush to the platform and many gave their donations, half-dollars, dollars, fives and many pledged other sums. The meeting was suspended. Some hurried home and returned with money, rings, watches, bracelets, etc. A total of $600 was collected and $200 more was realized from the jewelry. With the $800 they launched the "Forverts" ("Forward"). An appropriate sign was placed over the front of a rented store on East Broadway on the site of what is now Seward Park and opposite the present twelve-story Forward Building.

Pine, who Cahan, in his book entitled "Bletter Foon Mein Leben" ("Leaves of My Life"), described as the "leader of the kneepants makers union and one of the most active people in the Socialist movement, notes the appearance of the first "Forverts" (Forward) as follows:

"The first 'Forverts' was issued on April 22, 1897—a lovely spring day. I worked in a knee-pants shop on the Bowery and it arrived at the shop late in the afternoon. I kissed the new-born baby, pressed it to my heart, looked at the little letters but couldn't see them for my eyes were filled with tears. Aha, this is the spiritual child born in agony and pain. How thin! What poor blood it had! How weak this infant was! Can it live long? (The Forward just celebrated its Sixtieth Jubilee.) Joy overcame my tears and doubt disappeared. I could no longer sit at the machine and I put on my coat and out I went. Outside the shop youngsters were shouting, 'Forverts'—Extra —'Forverts.' Their voices sounded like sweet music to my ears. Joy was mixed with sadness for I felt that we soon would be left without a party for sooner or later we would be expelled from the Socialist Labor Party. The day was not far off. That fear became a reality that summer."

The United Hebrew Trades remained with the "Abend Blatt," published by the Arbeiter Zeitung Publishing Association, for the United Hebrew Trades was then in the hands of the DeLeonites. Max Pine and several others left the United Hebrew Trades as a result of the said split. Of course, Pine was back with the United Hebrew Trades soon enough and became its very great leader as mentioned previously in this book.

The DeLeonites then declared the Abend Blatt as the official daily of the Socialist Labor Party and thus the opposition could not fight the "Abend Blatt," without inviting the danger of being expelled from the party. Certainly none of the Forward people wished that. However, the opposition found a method of attack on the daily. They organized themselves into press clubs. All opposition was in the name of these press clubs. Thus the members could still remain in the party. The method worked as follows: They would hold a meeting of the Jewish Branch of the Socialist Labor Party and everything went well. After the S.L.P. meeting was closed, the same people would constitute themselves into a press club and then bitterly denounce DeLeon and his actions. They even collected money for the new daily, the ''Forward.''

Finally the ''Abend Blatt'' attacked them. DeLeon decided to expel them from the Socialist Labor Party. He first filed charges against Pine, Cahan and others, for breaking party discipline. These charges were referred to the grievance committee of the party and a trial was ordered.

Pine had high hopes that Alexander Jonas would not permit the expulsion, for expulsion, he felt, would be moral death for them.

Who was Alexander Jonas? When Pine first saw him, he became attached to him with all his heart. He was a German, clean-shaven, had bright eyes under his spectacles, was careful and wholesome, wore latest styled clothes, looked like an aristocrat, did not have a bit of haughtiness like DeLeon, was friendly to all. His smile won all. He came from a fine Berlin family, had private tutors and a good education. He liked the East Side Jew and the East Side Jew liked him, either because he was a refugee from the German Socialist Revolution of 1848, or because his gentle nature was sympathetic to the poor Jewish Immigrant. He joined them all in their large and small strikes; he spoke at their strike meetings, in his clear sympathetic voice.

The dispute among the Jewish socialists was distasteful to him because he was then the editor or co-worker of the German ''Volkszeitung.'' Pine hoped that since Jonas had great influence with the German Socialists who were then the mainstay of the Socialist Party, the expulsion would not take place.

Pine stated that they "banked on Jonas to help them for the following reasons: 1. DeLeon did not like him; 2. He agreed with us that we must combat the tactics of breaking up unions with all our might; 3. We thought his great sympathy for the Jewish masses would help us in our critical times. Jonas differed with us on the matter of a free press, for he feared that a free press would undermine party discipline in which he strongly believed. He defended us and wrote an article in our "Forverts" at great personal risk which was considered an insult to the Czar of the Socialist Labor Party, DeLeon."

However, DeLeon was more powerful than Jonas and DeLeon succeeded in his machinations.

The trial took place. Pine described it thus:

"The whole trial was a joke. They invited us just for the sake of the record and with the formality of a Russian Court. (History seems to repeat itself.)

"The trial hearing was held at the German Labor Lyceum. Waldinger, an old German-American and DeLeon's follower, presided. His demeanor was similar to that of a Russian judge or police official, (not unlike that of the O.G.P.U.).

"We, who were on trial, were angry and protested. There we met our Jewish 'Genossen' face to face. When we looked at them, they lowered their heads.

"One of the witnesses against us was Abraham Shapiro, the then secretary of the United Hebrew Trades. The DeLeonites had obtained control of the United Hebrew Trades and deposed Bernard Weinstein, one of its organizers because he showed sympathy towards us. It was this Shapiro who was one of the worst 'slaves to the bosses of the party.' He was most honest, punctual like an automaton and blindly devoted to the old regime like a soldier with a gun on guard. He was one of those who charged us with the betrayal of the interests of the workers and of the Socialist Party workers.

"Waldinger, who later also turned against DeLeon, was in the Judge's chair.

"With insolence he asked Cahan, 'What is your name?' We were all burned up at such arrogance and insolence. Our very beings revolted. Cahan, who was one of the most popular figures in the socialist world and particularly among the non-Jewish socialists, should be asked for his name!

"Cahan answered in Russian, 'It's none of your business; I have no passport.'

"Waldinger became angry: 'Here we speak the language of the United States.' (Cahan was also among the best English-speaking socialists).

" 'That you have to learn from me, since I am a teacher, Cahan shot back. This made us very happy.'

"The result of the hearing was that we were all expelled from the party. We were stunned; it was like sending us to the moral gallows.

"We did not long remain aimless. Soon we organized a party—Socialist Party—found a leader —Eugene V. Debs—and new hope. Our street was lit once again."

On October 5, 1897, there was published in the "Forverts" a letter from Max Pine, which read:

"Whoever thinks of the Socialist Labor Party of the last few years must come to the conclusion that votes were not lost by the campaign issues but were lost by the activities of the party itself because it undermined the fundamental principles of socialism. A labor party must be the guide and point out the way for the worker, not the person with a lash; a teacher, not a brand; the friend of the downtrodden, not the one to strike him down.

"When the typesetters will vote for the Socialist Labor Party after it made the effort to take from them their bread and butter; when the 'Genossen,' who did so much work for the organization and were united politically with the politician Bradley and Policeman Harns, will do likewise; when the tailors, cigarmakers and brewers, whom the party organ 'Alliance' tried to destroy, will do likewise, well and good. BUT NOT ME! For me, to help the Socialist Labor Party means to help the worst element of the proletariat. Those who see the Socialist Labor Party as the leader of the American people, don't see their own slow suicide."

It is important to note that actually these anti-DeLeonites were not expelled by the Grievance Committee. The committee merely reported to the Executive Committee of the party and recommended expulsion. When the Executive Committee met, the report of the committee was backed by DeLeon, but a motion to accept the report was actually defeated. There were enough level-headed "Genossen" in the party who agreed with Jonas and refused to expel the opposition. However, DeLeon tried another tack and ordered a Special Meeting of all party members for Sunday, July 25, 1897, when all of the Forwardists and anti-DeLeonites would be on the First Forward Excursion outing on the Hudson, so that none of them could be present at that meeting.

At that meeting, DeLeon proposed that all East Side Districts of the party be expelled. The motion was carried and, as Pine said: "We were left without a party. Morally, we were hit badly. We loved the Socialist Labor Party. It was the only beacon light and bearer of socialist thinking in America. It is true that the tactic was destructive, for the trick chased from its ranks American workers, and its leaders were tyrants. Still, it was the then only party of the workers. We then felt as if we were condemned to be hanged on the gallows."

Cahan describes the expulsion somewhat differently. He writes that the motion to expel the opposition did not pass. However, DeLeon then proposed that the party be reorganized and the branches improved. That motion was passed and by means of said reorganization, the opposition was expelled.

Fortunately for these socialists, along came Eugene V. Debs. At a Special Convention of the American Railway Workers Union held on June 15-21, 1897, he organized the Social Democratic Party. Pine and these Social Democrats who were soon thereafter expelled from the Socialist Labor Party joined forces with Debs and threw themselves heart and soul into the work of the new party. The Social Democratic Party became the Socialist Party in 1901.

Debs' first speech in New York was made on October 8, 1897. In the Forverts of October 9, 1897, there is found the following report:

"Last night a meeting was held in Bromers Park in Harlem, attended by six hundred, most Americans. Debs was the principal speaker and was greatly applauded. After a short introduction by Pine, a young American Socialist, Debs spoke about the fruits of American capitalism."

Pine devoted himself to the work of the party. He spoke, helped organize, ran for public office from time to time, but was never elected. The Socialist Party reached its heights in New York in 1914 when it elected Meyer London to represent the East Side in the United States House of Representatives.

Pine's attitude toward Russia and Communism is well illustrated by the following incident at an Arbeiter Ring (Workmen's Circle—a Fraternal Benefit Society) Convention. A resolution was introduced containing two parts. The first part called upon the League of Nations and the United States to recognize Soviet Russia. The second part required the Arbeiter Ring to join with the socialist movement of the world in demanding of Russia to give full freedom to all socialist political prisoners who, although on principle were against the regime, remain true to the working classes and did not join the counter-revolutionary forces against the Soviet government. The leftists bitterly attacked this revolution. Max Pine spoke forcefully in favor of it and said among other things:

> "*Being for Soviet Russia does not mean that we are for all the terrible happenings in Russia. We are not for the Tchreswitchaiky (O. G. P. U.). We also oppose oppression of press and assembly which the majority party uses against other parties.* 'Tis true, the Soviet leaders say this is all temporary; we believe them in that and we feel that the time has come when old injustices must be forgotten. The socialist revolutionaries and the Menshiviks have now put down their weapons, and therefore, they must be freed just as were freed those old counter-revolutionaries who took part in the uprising of Denikin and Koltchak.''

The resolution was adopted 100 to 40.

At a conference of the Socialist Democratic Federation there was held a discussion about communist influence in the Socialist Party. Max Pine, Secretary of the United Hebrew Trades, spoke against leaving the Socialist Party.

So did Alexander Kahn, representing the Forward. The motion was passed 41-33. The 33 opposition organized the Jewish Socialist Federation, the right wing of the socialist movement. They published "Der Wecker," a weekly, under the editorship of H. Lang.

When Abraham Cahan returned from Europe on September 10, 1921, he threw himself into the struggle against the communists, (who were formerly the DeLeonites), whom he called the enemies of labor and the Bolsheviks. Olgin, Dr. Hoffman (Zivion), Rogoff and others left the Forward with the left socialists. However, Rogoff and Hoffman later returned to the fold, the former as the managing editor of the Forward and the latter as a leading columnist, while Olgin became a leading figure in the group publishing the "Freheit", the Yiddish communist daily.

Pine remained affiliated with the Forward and with the Social Democrats until the end. He wrote numerous articles for the Forward and for the other socialist weeklies and monthlies.

It is interesting to note the comparison of the contents of a Yiddish daily with that of an English daily. Compare the contents of the Forward with that of the New York Times for the same date picked at random—October 3rd, 1958:

The Times contained the following features: news, local, national and foreign; book reports; editorials; a music and drama page; sports; financial reports; shipping and mail news; ads; analysis of the situation in the U. S. A. and the Far East.

The Forward of the same date had the following features: news, local, national and foreign; including a good deal about Israel and Jewish affairs; articles on the following subjects. Microfilming of the Yiddish Press; interview with Ben Gurion; report on the U. N. meeting; saving of an underground orphan hero from behind the Iron Curtain;

history of Yiddish theater and the Adler family; thoughts about the Sukoth festival; television programs—good or bad; biography of an important visitor from Israel; labor; editorials; chapters of three different novels; women's page; theatre and music news; radio and movies' page; letters to the editor; brief items about cantors; Jewish organizational life; advertisements.

The Day-Jewish Journal of the same day had the following features: news, local, foreign and national; including a good deal about Israel and Jewish affairs; articles on deGaulle; rabbinic problems; France-whither, Jewish life in Poland, racketeering, Sukoth, commentary on weekly bible reading, biography of a Herzl forerunner, Harriman's struggle for the Union Pacific; chapters of four novels, T.V. and radio programs; editorials; music and drama page; letters to editor; page on Jewish organizations; source material from the Talmud; advertisements.

Note, that the Yiddish daily is almost similar in content to the Sunday Times, which is a great adult educational institution.

The English newspaper readers have a large variety of books and magazines for educational purposes. In the case of the Yiddish reader, the daily is practically his only form of education. Almost all of the immigrants since 1897, the date of the founding of the Forward, have learned about Americanism, their problems and the problems of the world, its literature, drama, music, art—all cultural forms—from the Yiddish daily.

The Forward, which Pine helped to found, became the key to Jewish immigrant life in America and continued to be so throughout Pine's life and up to this very day.

Chapter 9

PEOPLE'S RELIEF COMMITTEE

The American theory of impregnability by reason of the two oceans left the American people complacent toward Europe during the period immediately preceding and during the early stages of World War I. The American Jews were somewhat affected by the same attitude toward their fellow-Jews in Europe. The East European Jews were considered by the Americans as persons to be pitied but their plight and problems were considered remote from American homes.

The immigrants who arrived here were helped considerably and they in turn helped their European brothers. The Yiddish press discussed the conditions in the homelands of the newcomers, but the older generations of Americans were untouched by these conditions, and in fact, ignorant of the problems which these conditions created.

The Kishineff massacres, followed by the great mass meetings of protest at Carnegie Hall on May 27, 1903 and similar meetings held throughout the United States, and the Russian pogroms that followed the abortive revolution of 1905, stirred the American people to action, but not on a permanent relief basis. These were merely warnings. But still, few Americans could imagine the misery and horror which World War I would bring upon the Jews of Europe. Few American Jews realized that those millions of East European Jews had two enemies to worry about in that great war; one at the front and the other behind the front.

American Jews had difficulty in realizing that while other war sufferers would turn to their fellow nationals for financial and moral support, the Jews could turn to no one except their far-off brothers in the Western Hemisphere. They did not realize that not only would there be physical suffering but that the spiritual life of these people also faced extinction, their synagogues, schools, press, books, stage and cultural organizations.

No doubt, specialists or professional Jews knew these things, but the ordinary Jew, the middle class, the shopkeeper, the manufacturer, the just plain Jew was hardly aware of the danger.

As the war gathered momentum, appeals for help came pouring into America. The Alliance Israelite of France and the Anglo-American Association of England asked their fellow wealthy and influential Jews of the American Jewish Committee for help in caring for the thousands of immigrants who were stranded in France and England on their way to America.

International organizations like B'nai Brith received calls for help from their sister lodges in Europe. "Landsmanshaften" received soul-stirring appeals from their "landsleit" in Russia, Bessarabia, Roumania, Poland, etc.

Orthodox organizations in the old country sent appeals to the Union of Orthodox Jewish Congregations and others here. Unions of Jewish workmen in Europe sent appeals to their fellow unions in the one land which could help them.

And so the appeals continued. Finally, as the result of these numerous and diversified appeals, three distinctly different relief organizations were created.

On October 14, 1914, the Central Committee for the Relief of Jews Suffering Through the War was organized by the orthodox synagogue group under the presidency of Leon Kamaiky, publisher of the "Tageblatt," the Jewish Daily News of New York, with Harry Fishel as Treasurer.

On October 24, 1914, the American Jewish Relief Committee was created upon response to a call from Louis Marshall, the Chairman of the American Jewish Committee. Marshall was made President and Felix M. Warburg was made Treasurer of the Relief Committee. Less than a month later these two relief agencies established the Joint Distribution Committee to distribute in Europe and Palestine the funds respectively collected by them.

Both of the above relief groups, however, failed to penetrate the great mass of the Jewish people not associated with the American Jewish Committee, the synagogues or congregations. The great masses were thus practically inactive in the matter of war relief. It was felt that the great masses, although poor, if once their interest and cooperation could be enlisted, offered untold possibilities. Finally, after a good deal of propaganda in the Forward and amongst the Jewish unions, and a great deal of work on behalf of the United Hebrew Trades, an organization conference was held at the Educational Alliance on August 8, 1915. A Committee of One Hundred and Ten was formed representing all groups of the "Yiddisher Gass," with one purpose—to help the Jewish war sufferers.

After preliminary sub-committee meetings, the first National Convention was held at Ford Hall, Boston, on the week-end commencing November 18, 1915. Calvin Coolidge, the then Lt. Governor of Massachusetts, greeted the Convention. The Credential Committee reported that there were present 121 delegates from 35 cities and in addition there were six delegates of the Committee of New York Volunteers; 8 from New York Workmen's Circle Branches, 1 from the Greater New York Ladies' Auxiliary. Louis Lipsky, Jacob Panken, Dr. Motzkin, and Joel Entin were among the members of the Resolutions Committee.

Meyer London, acting as chairman, opened the proceedings by saying among other things:

"What is the cause for Jewish suffering? Their complete devotion to idealism. Should the Jew wish to yield and disappear, completely assimilate,

he would not suffer. * * * Our relief is like a drop
in the ocean of need.''

Plans were devised to reach all Jews and to interest them
in its work. House-to-house canvasses were planned with
thousands of volunteers. A souvenir button was ordered.
It was a miniature reproduction of Jules Butensky's famous
statue ''Golut'' (Exile) which depicted a Jew with a child
in one hand, carrying a bundle in the other, wandering
forth, facing the storm that is tearing at his long coat.
The button became symbolic of the plight of the Jewish
people and became the symbol of union and sympathy between the American Jew and his brothers overseas. Thousands of these buttons were sold at $1.00 each.

The People's Relief Committee merged with the Joint
Distribution Committee for the purpose of distributing the
funds which it would obtain.

The organization later known as People's Relief Committee carried on an extensive campaign among the working classes, the professional men and women, and among
all elements and groups not then organized. It held a Tag
Day in New York on December 29, 1915. On January 27,
1916 collections were held throughout the country for it was
the declared Jewish Day. Almost $300,000. were raised
that day from pennies, nickels and dimes. Peretz memorial
meetings were held throughout the country on April 23,
1916, when more funds were collected. A successful Flower
Day collection was conducted on June 25, 1916.

The name of Jewish People's Relief Committee was
adopted at the third session of the Boston Conference
under the chairmanship of Louis Lipsky. They then also
adopted a declaration which contained among other things:

"The monies collected among the Jews in neutral lands for the Jewish people is not in any sense
charity or philanthropy. It is not help from an
individual to an individual, but is the natural and

organic effort of one part of Jewry for the historical self-sufficiency and dignity of the entire Jewish people.

"The monies that are being collected shall go not only for physical relief but also for spiritual sustenance of our people."

These policies were strictly adhered to.

By October 15, 1916, the Joint Distribution Committee had sent to Europe, Asia and Africa, $5,540,613.69 of which the People's Relief Committee contributed $606,094.06.

At the Second National Convention held on the week-end of May 30, 1918, at The Temple, Cleveland, Rabbi Abba Hillel Silver, the Rabbi of the Temple, greeted the delegates. He praised the People's Relief Committee for doing a wonderful job in destroying "Philanthropism" and substituting instead a spirit of brotherly responsibility.

Max Pine, then Secretary of the United Hebrew Trades, spoke at the opening session. He praised the spirit of the Jewish worker for his donation of one day's work for the relief. Pine also presided at the second session. Announcement was made that since the Boston Convention the People's Relief Committee raised $756,166.05 and that it contributed to the Joint Distribution Committee a total sum of $1,270,391.09 since its inception.

The Third National Convention was held on the week-end of November 8, 1919 at the Adelphia Hotel, Philadelphia, with Alexander Kahn in the chair. Baruch Zuckerman reported on behalf of the Administrative Committee. He submitted the reports of the delegations to Europe consisting of himself, Meyer Gillis and Max Pine. He described the extended tour of American cities made by Pine and Zuckerman on behalf of the Committee and how much additional work was done. Announcement was made that since the last convention $1,300,000 was raised by the Committee.

At the meeting of the Executive Board of the People's Relief Committee held on October 10, 1920, Baruch Zuckerman proposed that the Committee secede from the Joint Distribution Committee on the ground that the J. D. C. was strangling the Committee because it was not distributing its funds to educational and cultural institutions in Poland in accordance with the Committee's declaration above set forth. Pine argued against secession. Among other things he said:

"I was in Warsaw when the telegram arrived from the United States asking the workers if we should break with the J. D. C. That was a foolish request. We, the contented, ask of the tormented worker in Poland whether we should break with the J. D. C.

"I ask you friends, what can the People's Relief Committee, with its own meagre funds, do for so many children orphaned in the Ukraine pogroms.

"I say we cannot alone do constructive relief when little orphans in Pruskurov and Vitebsk sit on the bare earth and warm their little hands. * * * Now we must save people from death, and the J. D. C. had done proportionately one thousand-fold more than all others who came to the Carlsbad Conference."

The first vote taken showed a tie, twenty to twenty. A roll call was ordered and the vote was 21 to 19 in favor of the break. Then a resolution was adopted that a conference be called for November 13 and 14, 1920, at Philadelphia at which time the matter would finally be determined.

The Special Conference was held at the appointed time and place. The announcement was made that since the last convention the sum of $1,963.90 was received. Pine was chosen chairman for the second session at which the break with the J. D. C. was to be discussed.

After a heated and thorough debate a compromise was reached. The decision was that the People's Relief Committee demand of the J. D. C. that a portion of the funds contributed by the P. R. C. should be earmarked to help workers' institutions in the countries designated.

On June 26, 1921, a proposal was made to the Executive Committee that a delegation be sent to Russia to arrange for the relief of Jews in Russia. Baruch Zuckerman reported that the Administrative Committee felt that the People's Relief Committee could do most effective work in Russia because it represented American labor organizations. Some members felt that a mission was necessary because of the contradictory reports of the atmosphere behind the iron curtain. Others felt that since there was in Russia a Jewish Culture League, an impartial Socialist League doing cultural work, it would be better to communicate with them and to send money to the League. Another thought that the mission would be a failure because no proper committee could be obtained which could be effective there and have influence there, create an impression on Rusisa and also on the Jewish community here. Vladek argued for a mission for two purposes: 1. propaganda for Russia through a reputable person, one who could come back and gain the confidence of the people here and raise money; 2. to investigate and arrange for the sending of money to Russia. The motion was passed and the Administrative Committee was dirccted to determine the personnel of the delegation who shall be acceptable to the Executive and to the Russian Government.

The Administrative Committee chose Max Pine to go to Russia. The Executive Committee approved and the name of Pine was sent to the J. D. C., the group that was making all arrangements. The J. D. C. added the name of Judge Harry Fisher of Chicago to that of Max Pine and asked the Russian Government for visas for them. Approval came in due time and Pine and Fisher went off to Russia.

Upon their return Pine and Fisher reported as follows:

There were three classes of Jews who needed help in Russia: 1. those pogromized; 2. those residing in the cities at the front; and 3. war and civilian prisoners and refugees.

All Jews in the Ukraine suffered from the pogroms, directly or indirectly. They lived through a most brutal, bloody, murderous pogrom that started in December, 1918, and wasn't over yet. In some places the pogrom stopped but fear of resumption was in the air and Jews lived in constant fear.

The government in Ukraine was either incapable or unwilling to combat the gangsters and to protect the Jews.

Whether one agreed with the form of the Russian government or not, it would be an unpardonable sin not to openly declare the fact that Soviet Russia was the only power in East Europe, which earnestly, truly and ably took steps to do battle with those taking part in the pogroms and used its entire moral and physical power to destroy the monster known as ''pogrom'' which took possession of the ''white armies'' in the form of anti-Semitism. Every counter-revolutionary group in Russia bathed in guiltless Jewish blood. Every reactionary movement made its first objective a program of agitation against the Jews with circulars, bulletins and news articles. And, if Soviet Russia was blamed for its Red Terror, its action was like child's play compared with the action of its enemies.

With respect to the formerly oppressed peoples, the Soviet Government showed such a free and human spirit which could not be found in any other land in Central and East Europe. It was saddening to state that the allies entirely aided the enemies of Russia.

In this regard, even more striking was Russia's treatment of the Jews. Russia gave billions of rubles of relief and constant and humanistic assistance to the Jews, despite the fact that Jewish masses were anti-Bolshevik and opposed the government. It was important to note that the vast majority of Russian Jewry are Zionists and Zionists were declared to be counter-revolutionaries and their leaders were imprisoned.

The immediate future of the Jews in Ukraine seemed hopeless. Epidemics followed the pogroms. Jews left their all in the small communities and ran for protection to the large cities which were already overcrowded. Economically they were ruined, first by the pogroms and then by the official acts of the government. There was no means left to earn a livelihood. There was no clothing, no underwear, no shoes, no medicine for the sick. Everything needed for even primitive civilized life was missing. Commerce was at a standstill and there were no machines and tools to work with even where there was work to do.

By reason of the defeat of the armies of Koltchak, Yudenitch, Deniken, Momontov, Petlura and others, there was spread among the Russians a belief that it was God's revenge on all of those who shed Jewish blood, and that no government that was stained with Jewish blood could long endure.

How great was the Jewish wandering at the start of the war, from the Galician towns, from Grodno, Vilna, Kovno, and Courland States from which Jews were expelled in 48 hours after the start of the war. Those women, children and aged who survived spread out through the length and breadth of Russia, over the Urals and into Siberia. That happened when the men folk were in the trenches at the front offering their lives for the Czar's government. In addition, the leading Jews of the various communities were arrested and held as security. So, too, were the rabbis, intellectuals and merchants. They were torn from their families and homes.

When they were set free, they were beginning to wander about in the hope of finding their families and homes. Pine met many of these wanderers in Moscow. Terror overtook them upon meeting them; they looked weak and emaciated as if they were on their last breath. The Galician Jews were even worse off. It took them eight to ten weeks before they reached Moscow from Siberia and now they could not proceed further for the war was in their path. Of all the horrors seen on the trip through Russia nothing made a more terrible impression on Pine than the picture of these homeless people that were torn from their own for four or five years and anxious to learn if even one were alive, but could not proceed further in their search.

Luckily, Russia made a treaty with Lithuania and Latvia for the exchange of their citizens and about 200,000 Jewish refugees, war and civilian prisoners were being sent home. They were all in great need and looked to America as their only hope.

During this entire time there developed a real renaissance in Jewish cultural life. Yiddish and Hebrew culture, struggling against each other, both developed. Kiev seemed to become the center of Yiddish literary creation. There developed Yiddish art, music, drama, good and bad. The land was literally covered with a network of schools where both languages were taught. High schools and even the beginnings of Yiddish Universities were created in Moscow and Petrograd. Everywhere there were created teacher seminaries, clubs, libraries, reading rooms and newspapers in Russian, Hebrew and Yiddish.

At first the Bolshevik October Revolution had no effect on them and it seemed that the Jewish cultural streams became greater after the Revolution. But a few months passed and the entire picture changed. The Revolution dismembered the Jewish body just as it dismembered the Russian Imperial Government. Commerce ceased. The political problems of Poland, Ukraine, Latvia, Estonia were no longer similar. National autonomy was truly recognized in Soviet Russia. But at the same time there was appointed a Commissariat for Jewish Affairs. This Commissariat was at first intended to become the center of Jewish autonomy activities. But under a regime of a proletariat dictatorship the Jewish commissariat saw himself also as the representative of the Jewish proletariat and started to function accordingly. He fought everything that he thought to be "Bourgeoise."

For a short time the Jewish Commissariat did very little and the Jewish non-communist elements entirely ignored him. But it was not long before he started active work. Soon the Commissariat as well as the government were moving along lines destined to destroy the institutions which they declared to be enemies of the communist state.

The first thing the Commissariat did was to issue a decree which closed all Jewish central organizations. Then there commenced a series of attacks on the Zionists who were considered burgeoise nationalists in Russia. At first the attacks took the form of anti-Zionist propaganda in the press and other forms so as to make Zionist activity impossible.

The fact was that the activity of the Zionists was such as to compel the government to attack them. The day after the Bolshevik Revolution, the Zionist Organization adopted a resolution which opposed the Soviet regime and representatives were appointed to the Committee to Save the Fatherland and the Revolution. That was the All-Russian Anti-Bolshevik Committee. The Zionists issued a proclamation to the Jews of Russia that they should stand against the Soviet Bolshevik Regime. That resolution had not then been rescinded.

The Jewish Communists of the Commissariat moved into the field of Jewish cultural activities. All cultural institutions were closed down and all work was transferred to the said Jewish Cultural League. Yiddish was declared as the only language for Jews. It was illegal to teach Hebrew in schools to children under sixteen.

There was no question but that the Zionists were opposed to the Communist Party. But they, together with all other Jewish anti-Bolshevik parties later changed their positions and became loyal to the government in all respects. Loyalty to the government was obtained because of the expressed desire of the government to destroy all class distinctions and to give equal rights to all citizens. Those expressions were accepted as genuine and the activities of the government along those lines were proper and in accordance with those ideals and were in earnest. So they believed. This placed the Jew in a better position than he had been before in the entire East Europe.

The founding of the Moscow Relief Committee was an undertaking that was at first sight thought to be impossible for under the governmental system, there was no room for private philanthropic organizations. The principle that the government and the people are one and the same thing naturally places all communal activities in the hands of the government. That theory was successfully put into practice by destroying all private organizations and the Commissariat for Communal Relief took over the work of caring for the needy, helpless and dependents throughout the country without regard to religion or nationality. The government program thus became not only extraordinarily vast but also quite interesting. If one could criticize it, it would have been only because all this relief work took on a communistic character, which the government naturally approved.

Unfortunately, Russia found itself in such a position that this constructive program of the department could not be carried out. Much was done under trying conditions, particularly for Jewish pogrom victims. But the catastrophe that befell the Jews in the Ukraine was so great and so overwhelming that with the best intentions, the Government could not find a solution. Those in charge were overwhelmed with the urgency and vastness of the problem and the work which had to be done. Because of these facts alone, the hands of the Commissariat were hanging loose and little was being accomplished.

What was the Jewish situation in Russia upon Pine's arrival? What was the prospect of doing something for the sufferers? Upon his arrival, he found that all Jewish communal organizations were liquidated, except the three which gained great prestige for their services during the war, namely: "Yekopa," "Ort" and "Oze". The existence of these three groups was also a precarious one. They merely kept their offices open but the signs of their last breath were evident. All communal offices were declared illegal and were closed. The Zionist organization which had played a leading role in Jewish political life was declared to be counter-revolutionary and 107 delegates, among whom were the leading Zionists in Russia, who met at a conference in Moscow, were jailed and were awaiting the verdict of the "Tchresitcharko." The Ope and Tarbut, the most important cultural organizations of Russian Jewry were also declared illegal and their places were taken by the Jewish Cultural League, a purely Socialist Yiddish organization.

Under such conditions Pine had to at once see whether it was possible to bring some help from American Jewry. And, if so, how shall the relief be brought and how shall it be carried out and how shall it be distributed.

One thing was certain. The need was so great that it would have been just to stop relief work in other countries and to concentrate on the work there where the Jews were living in such a hell that by comparison the suffering in other lands was like paradise. Cognizant of that fact, the delegation determined that if it were only possible to create an organization that could bring relief to even a small portion of the sufferers, it should be done. But all work had to be done through those organizations which have already proven themselves capable of helping during those bitter years, and that work would be turned over to them only on condition that the Government would agree and promise to give needed transportation guaranteeing the security of the products that would be sent and guaranteeing free movement from place to place of those in charge of the relief.

This, of course, meant that the Soviet Government had to yield on one of its principles—namely, giving official sanction to private initiative and private communal work; in other words, to permit the existence in the Jewish community of an organization which was considered a bourgeoise world group. Of course, it was expected that the Jewish communists would oppose such a plan with all their might. But the delegation also felt that without the communists they could not even begin.

Here the delegation's own principles came into play. It came to Russia as the representatives of the Joint Distribution Committee and therefore felt responsible to American Jewry for what it would create there. The delegation had to take a middle course upon which all parties could get together. But to bring them together required tact and foresight. They decided to use all the human powers and qualities that its members possessed.

Upon the delegation's arrival, there came to it representatives from Kharkov, Kiev, Odessa, Yekatrinoslav, who brought gruesome tales about conditions in the Ukraine. They told that 150,000 children needed immediate relief. The government services with its relief and the children's colonies for Jewish pogrom orphans reached only 10% of the needy children. Thousands were sick and died for lack of medicines. Other thousands became sick for lack of clothing and lack of the minimum requirements for cleanliness. Thousands of women became infected with venereal diseases caused by the barbarians who raped them in the over 2,000 pogroms. There were no homes for these orphans, for the homeless children, for the aged and the weak, for the insane; no hospitals, no ambulances in which to remove the sick, no tools for the workers.

These representatives spoke in the name of all of these and implored the delegation of the great American Jewish Community to save them. The American delegation felt its responsibility becoming keener and sharper and determined that it must not fail because of the quarrels of the parties. Pine pleaded with these various elements not to make final decisions and not put obstacles in the delegation's path but to give it a chance to look around and become personally acquainted with the problem so as to more clearly understand what were the differences between these elements. Assurances were given the Russians that the delegation was entirely neutral in respect to their political differences and that it was there as the representative of American Jewry to help all regardless of political belief.

The delegation soon commenced conferences and discussions. Some started at 9:00 A.M. and ended at 3:00 A.M. Conferences were held in the offices of the "Yekopa" with such people as Rabbis Mazeh and Nurock, Drs. Gran, Pevzner, Arkin, Bramson, Messrs. Kring, Falk, Zalkin and Tcherikover—representatives of the "right wing." Conferences were held at the delegation's quarters with Messrs. Yaffe, Kagan, Motiloff, Abramovitz, Mazovietski and others, representing the "center", the Social-Democrats. At the Bureau of the Jewish Commissariat conferences were held with Dimenstein, Rafas, Esther, Weinstein, Litbakoff and others of the "left wing." Thereafter other groups came. All of these presentations made and advice given were contradictory, confusing, and seemed to further the delegation from its goal.

Little by little the situation became clearer and clearer. Quietly Pine prepared a plan that was thought to satisfy and unite all. During a heated discussion, the said plan was proposed at the first conference of all the organizations where each had two representatives (Oze, Yekopa, Ort, Culture League, Bund (left), United (left), Bund (right), Jewish Communist Party, and Poale Zion (right)).

The first reading of the plan caused a storm of protest from all sides. However, the delegation held its ground for it knew that none of those protesting had a plan of its own. It was suggested that a committee be appointed to study the plan. That was done. The delegation was invited by the committee to be present at its discussions. After a series of committee meetings, the plan was approved with slight modifications. The representatives reported the result to their respective groups and another general conference was held at which the plan was adopted. The result of this meeting was put down in the form of a contract protocol that the delegation made with the Russian Government.

The principal provisions of the contract which was signed by the Soviet Government and Max Pine and Harry M. Fischer, representing the J. D. C. in Moscow were:

"1. Relief to the Jewish pogrom victims is part of the general government relief to the victims of counter-revolution and pogroms.

"2. In order to best distribute the relief coming from America throughout the Soviet Republic, there was established a United Jewish Communal Committee of Representatives of Communal and Political Organizations working under the control of and in accordance with the laws of the Republic and in accordance with the plans and principles of general relief throughout the land.

"3. The committee shall consist of two representatives from the following organizations:

a. Yekopa; b. Ort; c. Oze; d. Cultural League; e. Bund; f. The United Jewish Socialist Labor Party; g. The Jewish Communist Party; h. The Central Bureau of the Jewish Section of the Russian Communist Party; i. Bund (Social Democrat); j. The United Jewish Socialist Party (Minority); k. Poale-Zion; l. Sotmas—Federation of Jewish laboring masses; m. The All-Russian Centre Committee of the Geverkshaften to create a close link between the committee and the Russian proletariat; n. The Jewish Commissariat—as ex-officio; o. The American Delegation has the right to send an American citizen as a representative to the Committee as well as to the Executive.

"4. The Committee shall elect from its members a presidium of eight persons, one representative from each of Oze, Ort, Yekopa, Culture League, Jewish Commissariat, Jewish Secretary of Russia in the Commissariat of Education, and the American delegate.

"5. The Presidium shall assign to each organization its duties in the work of relief. Ort will help organize industrial help. Oze will establish sanitarium, health institutions, kitchens, mobile units, children's homes and colonies.

"6. Wherever necessary local committees will be organized out of the local political and communal organizations.

"7. All such organizations and institutions that will be created by the Committee will function under the control of the Government, under its laws and will receive government aid. If found necessary, the Government may delegate the Committee's work to those organs of the government doing that work.

"8. Government institutions doing relief work for pogrom victims shall be considered in the distribution of help and are to receive clothing, shoes, medicines and other relief articles, just like the institutions in the Committee.

"9. All articles, shoes, clothing, medicines and so forth shall be sent to the Russian Red Cross for the Jewish Committee. They will be kept at Red Cross warehouses and will be released to the Committee upon request.

"10. The Government will facilitate the transportation of the relief goods and the movement of the personnel of the Committee; the Government guarantees the security of the goods and will guard same so that they will not be used for other purposes.

"11. The American Committee—the J. D. C.— agrees to give the Committee all material and financial help for pogrom victims. Should this not be carried out the agreement shall be void.

"12. Since transportation facilities in Russia are limited due to the blockade and since the transportation of relief material will further tax the already overtaxed railroads so that much material could not reach the needy in due time, it is hoped that the J. D. C. delegation will see to it that in addition to relief material they will also provide trucks that shall be used as a means of transportation."

The contract protocol was signed by the Russians as follows:

"Secretary of the Commissariat for Jewish Affairs—Mandelsberg; Member of the Commissariat—Dimenstein; Chairman of the Central

Committee of Russian Red Cross & Folks Commissar for Communal Affairs—Vinokurov—and the Secretary of the same Commissariat.

"This agreement was considered in Moscow as an historic document. The leaders of all the institutions hoped that with this contract would commence a new era for the Jews of Russia and the Ukraine."

The contract in short meant:

"Real relief work was transferred to Jewish communal organizations consisting of these three elements—Zionist, orthodox and conservative socialists. The control was placed in the hands of a presidium in which half of the leaders were from those organizations and half Communists. The work would be carried on in all of Russia, Ukraine and all sections affiliated with the Soviet Republic. They will control not only relief coming from the outside but also relief obtained from the Russian Government."

The delegation got more than it expected.

Pine was warned that it would be impossible to organize a Jewish relief committee that would concern itself with Jewish relief only. At the initial negotiations with the Russian representative Rakovsky at Revel for permission to come in and do its work, he was plainly told:

"Russia does not need philanthropy and will not permit a special Jewish activity because Russia does not recognize any differences between peoples and races."

Everyone with whom the delegation talked in Russia said it wouldn't get to first base. After all that warning the delegation felt very happy and proud, indeed, at the results accomplished.

To see these immediate results, it was but necessary to examine the government work for the victims at Borisov. While the delegation was in Moscow, it heard shocking news about pogroms in Borisov and other cities on the Polish border. The delegation obtained permission of the Russian Government to send an expedition there. Of its own meagre stores of clothing and medicines, the government filled two freight cars of things and dispatched them there with money that the delegation gave them for a month's work. Then came the news of Kiev and again the government dispatched immediate relief from the delegation.

It would only be fair to acknowledge the great work that the Soviet Government performed for pogrom victims even before the committee was organized. The government spent for such relief the unprecedented sum of 3,000,000 Rubles. And in order to avoid the anger of non-Jewish population for giving special help to Jews, the Government declared that these victims were the victims of the counter revolution. The fact is that anti-Semitism is considered counter-revolutionary. Criminals and anti-Semites were punished as such. The Government created colonies for Jewish pogrom orphans in those sections of Russia where there was more food. They were also taught Yiddish. These colonies were founded in regions far removed from the pogrom areas so that the orphans could forget those outrages that they lived through and to rehabilitate themselves.

After the contract was signed a constitution and by-laws were prepared for the Committee. The delegation found it necessary to appoint its representative one H. B. Eiserovitch, a former student at Petrograd University, a graduate of Voloszin Yeshiva, and a doctor from the University of Liege and University of Berne, and who spent the entire war period in relief work, and who also knew the problems and would work hard to keep harmony among the various elements of the Committee.

There remained several unanswered technical questions of the work that were also vital to American Jews. After a conference with Foreign Commissar Tchitcherin, the delegation left with him the following written questions:

"1. Do you guarantee that the Ukraine Government will accept the contract?

"2. What will be the method and rate of exchange for our money?

"3. How shall the money be sent?

"4. Can Americans send money directly to their relatives in Russia and the Ukraine? How, and under what circumstances?

"5. Can Americans and Russians send each other letters?

"6. Can those persons who are dependent upon their relatives in America leave Russia to come to America.

"7. How large is the number of Jewish war prisoners in Siberia?"

The answers received from Tchitcherin were:

"1. The Soviet Government undertakes to obtain the consent of the Ukraine Government for the work of the Committee.

"2. No reply.

"3. Already answered above.

"4. This is a complicated matter. According to law no private person can have more than 10,000 rubles. The Government agrees to pay to private persons at the rate of 1,400 rubles to the dollar.

"5. Postal exchange will be carried on.

"6 & 7. Answering the question you put to the People's Commissariat of Foreign Affairs on the possibility of uniting Jewish families that are living outside our land, permit me to advise you that all restrictions in this regard stem mostly from the restriction of traffic across borders made necessary in all countries carrying on wars as military necessities.

"The Central Committee for the evacuation of prisoners and refugees will be ready to commence discussions on the matter with you when you should deem it necessary to do so.

Respectfully yours,

N. Tchitcherin."

Pine reported that they could get no satisfactory reply while in Russia, because the official rate of exchange was 600 rubles to one dollar and 2,700 rubles to the mark. Finally, they came to an agreement with the Russian representative in Revel that for $75,000. that they could send the first month he would pay our committee about 150,000,000 rubles and thereafter for $50,000. a month he would give the committee as much as they will need even if they would be receiving at the rate of 5,000 rubles to the dollars.

Pine further reported that they weren't sure if the recipient of the money would not get into trouble.

All civilian and war prisoners who were in Siberia at the time of Koltchak's defeat, were freed by the Russian Government and received full rights of citizenship. Those desiring could go home. But most of them came from Galicia, a part of Poland then in Austria-Hungary, with whom Russia was then at war. It was, therefore, impossible for them to go home. Many of them were then working and living on a scale no worse than other Russians.

The Russian Government also contracted with the Latvian and Lithuanian Governments regarding the exchange of prisoners. Several hundred thousand Jews could thus leave Russia with almost no possessions because the most one could have on leaving Russia is 20,000 rubles, amounting to $7.00 and these would also look to American Jews for help.

The delegation would not complete its work without requesting the releasing of the imprisoned Zionists. The last of them were freed just two hours before Pine's departure, and they came directly from prison to bid the delegation farewell and to thank the J. D. C. and the American Jews.

Just before leaving Russia the delegation had the good fortune of receiving the glad tidings that the first transport of goods sent by the J. D. C. had reached Revel. The telegram was shown to all those interested. The first transport was considered by the Jews as well as the non-Jews of Russia as the first break in the iron curtain which cut off Russia from the outside world through the Blockade.

All those who first questioned the worthwhileness of the delegation's work were the first to come to it and declare their gratitude to it and to the Jews of America.

Pine asked the rhetorical question: "Will the Jews of America compensate that amount of gratitude by their giving?" In reporting the results of the trip, Pine said:

"Truly, we haven't done enough, that we should receive so much thanks and gratitude from those who have good reason not to trust the rest of the world. If it is the lot of Jews as a people to suffer, then the Russian Jews carry the suffering for all.

And for nothing, for a little sympathy, a little hope
do we buy from them all they have left.''

The delegation left Russia with the blessings of all
elements that couldn't get together till then. For the first
time since the Revolution they found a common ground
of activity. No one yielded on principle; no one left the
field for others. Their new activity was a new field—a separate field, a field saturated with the blood of the innocent,
shed by an enemy who made no distinctions between
classes and groupings of Jews. The murdering, the butcher-
ing, the plundering were all made in a democratic manner. All Jewish groups were equally represented in the
graves, insane asylums, in the masses of the suffering.
The painful shout that came from the countless victims
caused all to get together. It was the American Jewish
Relief delegation which was the magnetic instrument which
joined all.

Pine ended his report with:

''The prayers which they all send the American
Jewry is that the union, once established, shall
not be broken asunder.''

And so ended a great episode in the contract between
the East and the West.

GLOSSARY

BILUIM—a group of Russian students who emigrated to Palestine in 1882 and established the first colony named Rishon Lezion.

CHAZER MARKS—Yiddish for "pig markets".

DER YIDDISHER ARBEITER—Yiddish for "The Jewish Worker".

DIE FREIE ARBEITER SHTIME—Yiddish for "The Free Labor View".

DIE NAYE TSAIT—Yiddish for the "New Era".

FORVERTS—"Forward", a great Yiddish popular daily newspaper in America.

FREIHEIT—"Freedom", a left-wing newspaper.

GALUT—Wherever Jews resided outside of Palestine.

GENOSSEN—Yiddish for Socialists.

HISTADRUTH—General Labor Federation in Israel; an abbreviation for "Histadruth Haklalim Shel Haovdim Bayerets Yisroel".

KATERINKES—Yiddish for "playthings"—machines.

KEREN HAYESOD—Palestine Foundation Fund, the fiscal agent of the World Zionist Organization.

KEREN KAYEMETH—Jewish National Fund, the land purchasing and developing agency of the World Zionist Organization.

LANDSMANSHAFTEN—Yiddish societies named after the European towns the members came from.

MENDEL—Yiddish name for "Max".

ORT—Organization for the development of labor and craft among the Jews.

OZE—Russian Organization for the Protection of the health of the Jewish Community.

POALE ZION—Socialist Zionist group of the World Zionist Org.

SOTMAS—Russian Federation of the Jewish laboring masses.

STRIKE "HAGODOL"—The "great" Strike.

YEKOPA—Russian Jewish Relief Committee to aid War and Pogrom Victims.

YESHIVA "BOCHERIM"—Students of Talmud at East European schools, now destroyed.

ZAI ZAINEN NIT KAIN MENTCHEN—Yiddish for "They are not people".

ZUKUNFT—Yiddish for "Future".

PERSONALITIES

ARLOSOROFF, VICTOR CHAIM (1899-1933)—leader and one of the founders of the Histadruth.

BOROCHOV, DOV BER (1881-1917)—Theoretician and leader of the Poale Zion.

BRENNER, JOSEPH H. (1881-1921)—Hebrew Author and Palestine labor theoretician.

DEBS, EUGENE V. (1855-1926)—founder of the Socialist Party of the U.S. and perennial candidate for president.

FRIEDLANDER, PROF. ISRAEL (1876-1920)—scholar, educator, author, who, together with Bernard Cantor were sent to Europe by the American Joint Distribution Committee to help unfortunate Jews, both of whom were killed in the Ukraine.

GORDON, A. D. (1856-1922)—leader of Palestinian pioneers.

HAMLIN, ISAAC—Sec. of the Geverkshaften Campaign.

HERZL, DR. THEODORE (1860-1904)—Founder of the Political Zionist movement.

HILLQUIT, MORRIS (1870-1933)—Socialist attorney and labor leader and candidate of the Socialist Party for Mayor of the City of New York.

HIRSCH, BARON MAURICE DE (1831-1896)—He spent millions of dollars to settle Jews in Argentine and in Crimea but not in Palestine; refused to help Herzl.

KAHN, SHOLOM—instructor in English at Queens College, N.Y.C., teacher of Criticism of English Literature at the Hebrew University in Israel.

KATZ, DR. MORDECAI—famous East Side physician.

LA GUARDIA, FIORELLO—Member of the U.S. Congress and later Mayor of the City of New York.

LONDON, MEYER (1871-1926)—leading labor attorney and Socialist member of Congress.

MACDONALD, RAMSEY—Labor Party Prime Minister of Great Britain.

MARX, KARL (1818-1883)—Founder of the Socialist movement.

PANKEN, JACOB (1879-   )—Justice of the Domestic Relations Court of the City of New York, veteran labor attorney.

PERETZ, ISAAC LOEB (1851-1915)—a great Yiddish author.

POTOFSKY, JACOB—the successor to Sidney Hillman as president of the Amalgamated Clothing Workers Union.

RAMAZ, DAVID—leader of the Mapai, Socialist Labor Party in Israel.

REUTHER, WALTER—President of the United Automobile Workers and President of the C.I.O. and Vice-President of the A.F. of L. and C.I.O.; was seriously injured by a gun shot while he was at his home with his family, in an attempt to silence the labor leader forever.

ROOSEVELT, FRANKLIN DELANO (1882-1945)—32nd President of the United States, 1937-1945.

ROOSEVELT, THEODORE (1858-1919)—26th President of the United States, 1901-1908.

ROSE, ALEXANDER—President of the International Millinery Union and leader of the New York State Liberal Party.

ROSENFELD, MORRIS (1862-1923)—Yiddish poet of the proletariat.

SCHLESINGER, BENJAMIN (1876-1932)—former president of the I.L.G.W.U.

SCHNEIDERMAN, ROSE—former leader of womens' suffrage and trade union movements and Secretary of the N.Y. State Department of Labor.

SNOWDEN, LORD—former labor party leader.

WEDGEWOOD, LORD—leader of the British Labor Party.

WINCHEVSKY, MORRIS—considered to be the father, poet and philosopher of Jewish socialism.

ZELIKOWITZ, PROF. GETSEL (1863-1926)—also known as Goetsel Selikowitch—editor and scholar.

BIBLIOGRAPHY

American Federationist

American Federation of Labor Report of Proceedings at 35th Annual Convention at San Francisco, Cal. in 1915

American Federation of Labor Weekly

American History—David S. Muzzey

Ardent Eighties and After—Gregory Weinstein

Bilder Fun Yiddisher Arbeiter Bavegung in America (The Jewish Labor Movement in America)—Bernard Weinstein—1935

Bletter Fun Main Leben (Leaves from my life story)—Abraham Cahan—1926

Book of Exile—published by the People's Relief Committee, New York, 1916

Challenging Years—The Life of Dr. Stephen S. Wise—1949

Daily News—A New York City daily newspaper

Fertel Yorhundert Histadruth (Quarter Century of Histadruth)—Edited by L. Shpizman

Forverts (Forward)—A New York City Yiddish daily newspaper

Fuftsig Yor Cloakmacher Union (Fifty Years Cloakmaker Union)—Dr. B. Hoffman, 1936

Fuftsig Yor Geverkshaften (Fifty Years Geverkshaften)—1938

Fur and Leather Workers Union—Philip S. Foner, 1950

Geschichte Fun Arbeiter Ring (History of the Arbeiter Ring—A Fraternal Benefit Society) on the occasion of the 25th Convention—A. S. Sacks, 1925

Geschichte Fun Forverts (History of the Forward)—Osherovitch

History and Problems of Organized Labor—Frank Tracy Carlton

History of the Cutters' Union—Revised Edition—James O'Neil, 1920

History of the International Ladies Garment Workers Union—Louis Levine, 1924

Immigrant Invasion—Frank Julian Warne, 1915

Immigration and Law—Isaac A. Hourwich, 1912

Jewish Labor Movement in New York City—William M. Leiserson, 1924

Kapay Yeidioht (Hebrew Weekly, Tel Aviv, Israel)

Leben Fun Yiddishen Arbeiter (Sketches of the Life of the Jewish Workers in America)—Published by the Future Press, 1935

Memoirs of an American Jew—Philip Cowan, 1932

Minutes of the United Hebrew Trades

Morgen Journal (Morning Journal), a New York City Yiddish daily newspaper, now merged with the Day-Morning Journal

Political Social History of the United States—A. M. Schlesinger

Preliminary Report of the New York State Factory Investigating Committee, 1914

Reminiscences of the Cloakmakers and Other Unions—A. Rosenberg

Report of the Industrial Commissioner of the State of New York, Vols. 15 and 19

Rise of the Clothing Workers—a pamphlet—Joseph Schlossberg, 1921

Should a Charter be Issued by the A. F. of L. to the Central Labor Federation of New York with Socialist Labor Representation there?—a pamphlet issued by the American Federation of Labor, 1890

Spotlight on a Union—Donald B. Robinson, 1948

Sweatshops—an article by McLean in the American Journal of Sociology, Nov. 1903

Symposium—William English Walling, 1938

Tageblatt, Der (The Daily News)—a N.Y.C. Yiddish daily, first merged with Morgen Journal and then with the Day

Tailor Strike, The—B. Levitin

Teg Vos Zainen Shoin Lang Avek (Days of Long Ago)—an article by Max Pine

This Thing of Giving—Henry H. Rosenfelt, 1924

Times, The—a N.Y.C. daily

Tog, Der (The Day)—a N.Y.C. Yiddish daily newspaper

Tribune, The—a N.Y.C. daily

United Hebrew Trades Testimonial Journal in Honor of Morris C. Feinstone, 1935

Universal Jewish Encyclopedia, The

Wecker, Der—the I.L.G.W.U. magazine

With Firmness in the Right—Cyrus Adler and A. M. Margalith

World, The—a N.Y.C. daily newspaper, now merged with the World-Telegram

Yiddishe Almanac, Der (The Jewish Almanac)—edited by Victor Mirsky, 1922

Yiddisher Arbeiter, Der—a weekly magazine

Yiddishe Unions in America—Bernard Weinstein, 1929

Zait, Die (The Times)—a Poalei Zion paper

Zionist Movement, The—Israel Cohen, 1946

Zukunft, Die (The Future)—a Socialist daily

INDEX